123 WAYS

—— TO ADD ——

PIZAZZ

—— TO A ——

PANEL DISCUSSION

KRISTIN ARNOLD

QPC Press

Published by QPC Press
Scottsdale, Arizona

For ordering information or special discounts for bulk purchase, please contact
QPC Press at 28150 N. Alma School Parkway, Suite 103-616, Scottsdale, AZ 85262, 800.589.4733.

First printing 2020
ISBN: 978-0-9676313-8-7
Library of Congress Cataloging-in-Publication Data
1. Business communication
2. Business presentations
3. Public speaking

Disclaimer

This book is designed to provide basic information about panel discussions. It is not the purpose of this book to reprint all of the information that is otherwise available on the vast subject of panel discussions, but to complement, amplify and supplement other professional journals and books. You are urged to read other available references, learn as much as possible about panel discussions and tailor the information to your individual, team and organizational needs.
The author and QPC Press shall have neither liability nor responsibility to any person or entity with respect to any loss or damage caused, or alleged to be caused, directly or indirectly, by the information contained in this book.
If you do not wish to be bound by the above, you may return this book to the publisher for a full refund.

CONTENTS

FOREWORD

Panels are one of the most widely used session formats at meetings and conferences. Often viewed as the simplest and quickest format for assembling the conference program, panels put the "kids in the show" and can be helpful for boosting attendance.

In the past, a panel of experts was popular because the knowledge and wisdom gap between the stage and the audience was steep. Over the past ten years, that gap has significantly narrowed. Instead of focusing on loading up with experts, audiences value panels that bring something unexpected including diversity of thought and opinion.

When it comes to consuming meeting content, audiences have a much more sophisticated palate. Whether your next panel is digital or in-person, audiences are going to respond best to thought-provoking, future-leaning, and unpredictable social learning experiences.

And when it comes to panels, Kristin Arnold is the master. For over a decade, she has carefully studied panel session design and moderation. Under the brand *Powerful Panels*, she has created and shared informative articles, videos and podcasts to help panels "up" their game. Kristin is so obsessed with this topic, she started a LinkedIn Group (Powerful Panels) for industry professionals to share their ideas and pose questions. My company, Velvet Chainsaw Consulting, consider Kristin as our "go to" resource for inspiring our customers and team to raise the bar to make panels more exciting and informative.

Kristin has filled the pages of this book with ideas and inspiration to help you shake things up and better deliver value to your attendees. With the growth in virtual content consumption and delivery, these "next" practices have never been more timely.

> **PANEL ORGANIZERS** will up their game by more carefully selecting moderators and panelists and applying new techniques to traditional panel formats. The ideas in this book will challenge them to think differently about the session flow and design.

> **MODERATORS** will be inspired to completely rethink their approach to moderating a panel discussion. They can flip through the book and select a few techniques to create an amazing experience for the audience.

> **PANELISTS** will realize they can have a meaningful conversation. They will be encouraged to join an "unplugged" conversation that audiences will lean in, listen to, and learn valuable insights.

> **AUDIENCES** will be pleasantly surprised at the panel dynamic. As soon as they walk in, they will immediately notice that this panel will *not* be like other boring panels. They will appreciate a session that engages them as opposed to making them passive participants.

Consider this book to be your reference guide—chock full of ideas to take your panels from boring to extraordinary. Keep it close, refer to it often, and listen to your audiences rave about your panel being the hit of the conference.

Dave Lutz, Managing Director
Velvet Chainsaw Consulting
Winter Garden, Florida

PREFACE

Love 'em or hate 'em; panels are a prevalent meeting format and they are here to stay, even in the virtual environment. For the most part, audiences don't have high expectations, but they still come to a session with hopes of a "Wizard of Oz" moment where the curtain is pulled back on a topic. They are hoping the panelists will actually share their wisdom and insights. That there will be an element of surprise, of diverse viewpoints and provocative thinking. That it will be spontaneous and unscripted.

An audience wants to hear an up-close and personal discussion among panelists. They want the gritty part of the story not found on Google, YouTube, or TED.

The audience wants to lean in to hear what panel members say. They want to be challenged, and they want to observe how panelists disagree with each other as well as how they learn from each other.

People want to see more of these kinds of panel discussions at meetings, conferences, and conventions. That's why I was asked to write this book. Once you've learned the basics of moderating a panel (check out my book *Powerful Panels: A Step-by-Step Guide to Moderating a Lively and Informative Panel Discussion*), then it's time to add a little pizazz to your panels.

My fervent hope is that this book will inspire you to upgrade your panels. Use this book as your quick reference guide. Just flip through the pages. Some techniques will readily resonate with you, your panel topic, and the audience. Others may not apply at all…and that's perfectly okay. All you need is *one* new technique to add to your next panel discussion that will make it the hit of the conference!

January, 2021   Kristin J. Arnold
                                                                                        Scottsdale, AZ

INTRODUCTION

Harry A. Overstreet, an American educator, first coined the term "panel discussion" in a short article "On the Panel" in the October, 1934, issue of *The Trained Nurse and Hospital Review*. In essence, Overstreet envisioned panels as a "glorified conversation [with] all the delight of generous give-and-take. And if it is a genuinely good conversation, it sends people away with a warm feeling not only that their own ideas have been clarified but that their understanding of other points of view has been broadened."

The actual mechanics of a panel discussion at that time were to:

SET THE STAGE. "The members of the panel (usually not more than eight) sit on the platform, behind a long table facing the audience, so that they may comfortably lean forward as they engage in the discussion."

HAVE A CHAIR. "One member of the panel serves as chairman. His function is to state the problem and to keep the discussion well within the areas of relevancy."

HAVE NO SPEECHES. "If he is a wise chairman, he announces at the beginning the one simple rule of the procedure; that no one, under any circumstances, is to rise and make a speech. To do so, he indicates, will be the one unforgivable offense."

KICK IT OFF. "Informally introducing the individual members of the panel, he then states briefly the problem of the evening and throws the discussion open to the panel, inviting any member to speak as the spirit moves him."

NOT REHEARSE. "A nervous chairman will feel that something in the nature of a program must be agreed upon beforehand. He will therefore gather his panel about him and conduct a kind of preliminary discussion. No worse procedure can be imagined. The stimulation and the intellectual value of the panel method lie in its sheer spontaneity, for it is in the atmosphere of spontaneity that the best flashes of insight frequently come, the most fascinating turns of thought, the quips of humor."

ENGAGE AUDIENCE IN Q&A. "Usually, at the end of an hour or so—or better, when something in the way of one or more clear-cut opinions has shaped itself in the panel—the discussion is thrown open to the audience. It is most interesting to watch the swift response. The audience have thus far had no chance to express themselves. But they have been literally sitting on the edges of their chairs. When their chance comes, therefore, they are instantly on their feet. Usually from all over the room, questions and opinions come like rifle cracks, and for another hour the discussion waxes warm."

While the mechanics are still basically the same, a few modern updates are necessary to keep Overstreet's model current, and that's the purpose of this book. This book is designed to spark your imagination and creativity—to add a little pizazz to your panel discussion at your in-person, virtual, or hybrid meeting. Rather than relying on the one or two techniques you (and most panel moderators) seem to use, you have in your hands a wide-ranging smorgasbord of ideas and techniques you can use today to make your current panel discussions more lively, engaging, and interactive.[1]

---

[1] I warn you, though. This is <u>not</u> a basic panel moderation book (Oh! That would be my book, *Powerful Panels: A Step-by-Step Guide to Moderating a Lively and Informative Panel Discussion at Meetings Conferences, and Conventions.*)

Over the years, I've talked to a gaggle (which is not quite a google) of meeting planners about what makes a panel discussion successful. I've boiled it down to four basic criteria. By ensuring you have these four items, your panel discussion will be the hit of the conference. Miss one, and it will be okay but nothing remarkable or memorable. Miss two and you won't surprise anyone, since audiences don't have high expectations of panels. Miss three or four and you'll have a total snoozefest.

At the very least, you MUST:

1. **DELIVER ON THE PROMISE.** Whatever is stated in the promotional marketing materials, conference brochure, or meeting app, you must deliver on that promise.

2. **HAVE SCINTILLATING, SPONTANEOUS CONVERSATION.** The panelists should be engaged in an interesting discussion that is not otherwise available on the Internet. Audiences want to get a glimpse of a conversation that no one else has access to.

3. **PROVOKE DIFFERENCES OF OPINION.** It's boring to hear panelists say, "Yep, I agree with you." Why bother to attend the panel if everyone agrees on what to do? The most interesting panel discussions are set up to showcase the differences of opinions – between the panelists and how the audience is thinking.

4. **PROVIDE TAKEAWAY VALUE.** Even though the audience is witnessing an interesting and entertaining conversation, if they don't walk away with some relevance to their own personal or professional lives, why attend?

If you do it with a little pizazz, so much the better. Diana Vreeland, fashion editor of *Harper's Bazaar,* coined the term "pizazz" in the 1930s to mean an attractive combination of vitality and glamour. A panel discussion with pizazz – vitality and glamour – will make your audience lean in and listen.

All of these tips and techniques can be done in live, face-to-face (F2F) meetings. But don't let that limit your imagination! Use these ideas as a springboard to unleash your own creativity. While all of these techniques are equally applicable to the virtual world, some require a bit of tweaking. Where appropriate, I've added additional ideas under Virtual Variations to help you make those adjustments as well as a dedicated chapter on virtual panels.

Virtual variations will stand out
in boxes like this one.

Yes indeed, panels can be boring and lackluster, but they don't have to be. This book provides meeting organizers, panel moderators, and panelists specific ways to add vitality and glamour any panel discussion, which will make them the talk of your meeting, conference or convention.

PART ONE

PREPARE

TO

MODERATE

A

PANEL DISCUSSION

CHAPTER ONE
JUST FOR MEETING ORGANIZERS

Based on the meeting sponsor's vision and direction, the panel moderator brings that session to life by selecting and prepping the panelists, determining the format to ensure a lively and informative conversation and having excellent facilitator skills to keep the conversation focused and moving along.

~ Kristin Arnold

I WAS TALKING WITH A CEO of a large association about speaking at an upcoming convention when I mentioned that I also moderate panel discussions. She replied, "You know, I'm not a huge fan of panels." Upon further questioning, she said, "It all boils down to the moderator, and most of them just don't know how to facilitate an energetic, lively, and meaningful panel discussion."

I agree. It's crucial to engage a skilled facilitator who can tee up the topic and create a format for a behind-the-scenes feel that the audience can't get anywhere else. Based on the meeting sponsor's vision and direction, the panel moderator should bring that session to life by selecting and prepping the panelists, determining the format to ensure a lively and informative conversation, and having excellent facilitation skills to keep the conversation focused and moving along.

Facilitating a panel discussion is not easy. The panel moderator must master the art of multi-tasking by:

- Deeply listening to the current discussion and taking notes.
- Thinking through the overall planned discussion.
- Watching the time, controlling the length of the current discussion.
- Balancing the participation of panelists.
- Watching the reactions of the audience to extend or shorten current discussion.
- Deciding where to take the conversation next.
- Thinking about key points to summarize.
- Bridging between segments.
- Keeping the needs of the audience ALWAYS at the forefront.
- And most important, be interested in what the panelists are saying.

Yes, indeed. It's not easy to moderate a panel discussion. When done well, it's masterful, so be thoughtful about whom you choose to be your panel moderator.

FIND A SKILLED PANEL MODERATOR

I'm astounded to hear meeting organizers tell me they rarely vet panel moderators. They typically find a panel moderator by asking:

- A local celebrity, such as a newsperson.

- A well-known member of the association.

- A good sponsor who needs a little visibility to be happy.

- A colleague who offered to put together a panel.

- An associate who mentioned a certain person would be a good moderator.

- Google "who can moderate a panel".

- One of the speakers to do it.

- No one to moderate the panel, thinking a great conversation will spontaneously happen.

Next time you want to engage a panel moderator, perform the same kind of due diligence you would for your main stage keynoter:

ASSEMBLE A LIST of potential candidates—and don't forget to aim high! It's great to Google the usual suspects, but you can also work with a reputable speakers bureau to help you find just the right fit for your audience. (Full disclosure, I'm available on that list.)

CHECK CREDENTIALS. Have they ever moderated a panel before? Just because they're nice or a famous person doesn't mean they have the skills to facilitate a robust panel discussion.

VERIFY. Beware of people you *think* should be able to facilitate a conversation; they may be fabulous at reading from a teleprompter and lousy at impromptu performances. Ask for and check their client references and see if you can catch them in action. Do they have videos uploaded on YouTube? How interactive are they? Is the tone conversational? Is this person going to be effective with your audience?

SEE IN ACTION. If possible, observe the person in action at an upcoming event. Sometimes, that's just not possible (distance gets in the way or the other client doesn't want you to listen in), but it never hurts to ask.

LISTEN TO YOUR INTUITION. If it's hard to find good video or to see them in action, then rely on your intuition using a few indicators of success:

- When you initially call to see if they are available, they should ask *good, open-ended questions* about the program, the objectives, the people in the room. They should probe deeper where appropriate—don't be surprised if some questions make you think. That's what good facilitators do.

- When you ask about their experiences, they are able to *share several instances* where they moderated a panel before—possibly with the same kind of audience. When a moderator is able to rattle off several similar experiences, you know they've facilitated more than one or two a year!

- Ask them what kind of *preparation* they typically put into moderating a discussion. Listen carefully for cues that they will be attentive to the real issues your audience cares about. For example, will they research the topic? Reach out to your panelists to identify key issues? Interview a sample of the attendees? Post on social media to get a sense for the real concerns? If they say "I don't do much of that," take a pass. They may be a font of information about a topic, but they'd be better as a panelist than as a moderator.

- Ask them about how they would go about *engaging and involving* the audience. You're looking for more than Q&A at the end. See what innovative options your moderator offers.

- They should enthusiastically support the use of the official event app for conducting online polls, crowdsourcing questions, sharing panelist slides, etc. If you don't have an event app, a savvy panel moderator will share ideas on how to bring technology to the event if appropriate.

Just like speakers, panel moderators should add more value than just moderating the panel. They can engage the audience beforehand and reinforce key messages after the event. You have way too much at stake to allow just anyone to moderate your panel discussions. Before you say, "Yes" to that usual suspect, check them out. You'll have a higher probability of making your panel extraordinary.

> Make sure your panel moderator has some experience moderating a virtual or hybrid panel discussion. Don't forget to ask about their experience using various digital platforms—including the one you'll be using.

GIVE THEM A REASON TO SAY YES

Much of the time, a meeting organizer will ask a skilled facilitator to moderate a panel for free or for expenses. Unless the potential moderator sees the benefits, they will probably say, "No, thank you!"

Yet there *are* significant benefits and advantages for a moderator to agree to moderate a panel discussion. Small business expert and panel moderator Mike Periu outlines some of these benefits:

STAND OUT. "Few people have the chutzpah to stand in front of an audience of industry peers and orchestrate a meaningful discussion among experts. The sheer act of taking this responsibility on will help you build a name for yourself in the industry and/or company."

MEET INFLUENCERS. "In order to run an effective panel discussion, you need to find excellent panel candidates. You may have to go through a long list of people to find those who are able to do it, available to do it, and willing to do it. In the process, you could easily contact ten or fifteen industry heavy weights. They'll take your call because you aren't asking them to buy anything."

GET SMART. "It forces you to get up to speed on important industry issues...You have no choice but to dedicate time to it."

REACH NEW CUSTOMERS. "It gives you a great reason to reach out to new and potential customers when you invite people to attend a panel discussion to let them know how it went and summarize the key points discussed. These are two valid and interesting reasons to communicate with your audience."

CREDIBILITY/PRESTIGE. "There's just something about being up on stage that sends the message that you are someone with whom to do business. Most people are terrified of being on a panel, not to mention moderating one."

SHOW EXPERTISE. Denise Graveline adds, "As a featured performer on the panel, moderators will miss out on this bonus if they simply stick to reading the panelists' names and asking "any questions" at the end. Instead, smart panel moderators insert a comment here and there to sum up the sense of the panel, add a choice piece of data to illustrate what two panelists just touched on, and ask blunt questions that get to the heart of the matter...and ask unusual questions. Don't waste this opportunity!"

APPRECIATION. Barry Eisler says, "If you do a terrific job as moderator by bringing out the best in the panelists, the audience will appreciate you. They'll remember your name and buy your books. Being a moderator is actually a great sales opportunity—but only if you do it right" [in service of the audience].

AWARENESS. Mark Suster points out, "People at the conference become aware of who you are...it serves as a great conversation piece to meet people the rest of the conference. People will say, "Oh, I saw you moderate that [great panel discussion]." It's a free icebreaker during the rest of the conference!"

STEPPING STONE. Most importantly, moderating a panel discussion helps a speaker get ready for bigger speaking opportunities.

Obviously, there is a HUGE upside to saying "Yes". When you do a great job, you can come out looking like a rock star. Truth be told, this is partially true because there are so many bad moderators out there and people walk into a panel discussion with fairly low expectations. Imagine their surprise when they see a skilled moderator keep the conversation focused and lively! Even so, there is an equally HUGE downside to saying "Yes" if you are not willing to put the work into it.

Panel moderators should say "Yes" only when they see a worthwhile upside and are willing to put the work into making the panel discussion simply amazing!

WHEN TO GO PRO

When the stakes are high and you really need to hit a home run, you'll want to hire a *professional* panel moderator to:

INCREASE YOUR ODDS. 68% of all panels are considered merely okay or worse. Increase your odds of success by using a professional who has *been there, done that.* Of course, there's no guarantee, so just like hiring a professional speaker, do your due diligence; make sure the person you hire can actually do the job.

BREAK THE MOLD. Panel discussions tend to follow the same old boring, traditional format behind a white, draped table. Your professional moderator should have an extensive playbook of techniques to add pizazz to the process. A professional panel moderator can help shape the session with suggestions on the room set and creative panel formats that your attendees will rave about throughout the conference.

HAVE BETTER TAKEAWAYS. A moderator is a champion for the audience—making sure panelists stay focused on clear takeaways for the audience. A panel moderator is NOT an expert in the topic and therefore won't get sucked into dominating the panel or advocating for a specific position. The moderator makes sure the panelists look clever and the audience gets their key questions answered.

SELECT BRILLIANT PANELISTS. Unfortunately, not all panelists are spectacular speakers in front of an audience. A skilled facilitator can work with even the most boring expert to sound brilliant, and be fascinating.

BE ON TIME. Managing time is one of the top panel discussion challenges. A professional moderator, will start and end on time, use the time in between efficiently and effectively, and maximize the value to your audience.

BE LESS STRESSED. You'll know you're in good hands. You won't have to worry about a good job (or not). You can focus on bigger issues, knowing the moderator is carefully attuned to all aspects of session.

In the big scheme of things, when you factor in the direct and indirect costs of your meeting; hiring a professional panel moderator is a great investment in securing a successful panel discussion that is the highlight of your conference.

CHIT-CHAT YOUR VISION

Once the panel moderator has been identified, the meeting organizer and panel moderator should have a discussion about what the panel *could* be. What kind of pizazz are you looking for? What will fit best for *this* audience?

Some key items to discuss are:

THE EVENT. The panel discussion is typically one session within an entire event. Share the panel date, start and end times, and location. Also discuss where this panel is within the arc of the entire event agenda, what comes before and after. Discuss the desired goal(s) and outcome(s) of the session and overall event. Share the event website, marketing materials, theme and any other logistical information.

PANEL TITLE. An intriguing title will capture your audience's attention. Brainstorm ideas to develop a catchy and effective title consistent with the event theme.

PANEL OBJECTIVES. Clarify the stated objectives for the panel, especially if marketing material has already been published. What are the key messages and content that needs to be conveyed and explored? What do you want them to know, think or feel about the topic?

PANEL FORMAT. Discuss your vision for the panel. How formal or informal? Traditional or more unique? Confirm how much latitude you have to play with the format and agenda.

SPONSORING ORGANIZATION. Review their mission and ask about their past experiences with panels discussions—the good, the bad, and the ugly.

AUDIENCE. Confirm the audience size, demographics and expectations for the discussion.

- What's the expected level of expertise in the room around the panel topic?
- Key interests, needs, concerns, and expectations?
- What questions do they have?
- What impact could the panelists' comments have on their work and lives?

PANELISTS. Share the name, bio and contact information for any panelist confirmed to participate, why they were selected, as well as a copy of what has been communicated to them. Determine if there are any promotional policies or prohibitions you need to be aware of.

TECH-SAVVY. How comfortable are the speakers, moderators, panelists and audience members? Have they used technology or meeting apps in the past?

SUCCESS CRITERIA. Discuss how you'll determine and evaluate the success of the panel. Evaluation forms? Hallway buzz?

ROOM LOGISTICS. Share any details you have about room size and layout, furniture setup, and color of the backdrop. Explore the ability for the venue to change or alter the room and to turn the room for the next scheduled session.

AUDIO/VISUAL. Discuss audio (microphones), visual (video) and internet (Wi-Fi) requirements.

DRESS CODE. Confirm what the audience will be wearing. Be specific; not everyone has the same definition of business casual.

RIGHTS. If the panel will be recorded (audio and/or video) or live-streamed, you'll need the moderator and panel to sign a release form.

SUPPORT STAFF. Agree on any additional support needed in the room such as room monitors, microphone runners, or other volunteers or staff.

PROMOTION. Ask your panel moderator to help get the word out as well as any post-event messaging to reinforce the panel discussion.

As you discuss these items, you will have the opportunity to create an amazing experience for the audience and the panelists. When you make intentional choices, you greatly increase the probability that your panel discussion will be a home run. Use this checklist and resources to help the conversation move along.

www.PowerfulPanels.com/BONUS

Schedule a meeting with your panel moderator and A/V crew to identify and agree on the technology that will be used. Check out Chapter 13 for more information on virtual panels.

THE BENCHMARK FOR ALL PANELS

San Diego ComicCon (SDCC) is the ultimate panel discussion event of the year, packing Hall H with over 6,500 people (many of whom stand in line overnight) to hear from their favorite actors, programs, and authors. What's even more crazy is that the panel format is the dominant session format. Who knew panels were so attractive to audiences?

Wow! Can you imagine 6,500 people lining up for *your* panels?

Even SDCC is fearful of the panel format getting stale. WIRED author, Angela Watercutter said, "Call it prestige convention programming. As the outcomes of Con panels become more and more predictable—or in the case of shows like *Twin Peaks* and *Stranger Things*, more opaque because of the mysterious nature of their subject matter— a compelling moderator can keep things from getting stale."

Most of us are not organizing or moderating a panel at SDCC. But we can learn from "the best" and try something that will make our panels:

MEMORABLE. Ask, "What would be a memorable moment, story, or sound bite that would grab the attention of my audience?"

EXCLUSIVE. Ask, "What can I do for my audience that they haven't seen before?" *Hunger Games* fans were treated to an exclusive video message from District 13 that featured heroine Katniss Everdeen in a red, armored outfit.

LEADING EDGE. Ask, "What don't they know that they would *want* to know?" Halle Berry leaked the news that Jeffrey Dean Morgan was "going to swap fluids" with her during the current season of the show *Extant.* "Let's just get it out there," the actress told the cheering crowd.

BEHIND THE SCENES. Ask, "What about the process, the evolution, or the current state is baffling to the audience?" During a panel on fan fiction (fanfic), attendees got a glimpse into the writing process and the evolution of fanfic into mainstream culture. Anna Todd, (author of the wildly popular *After*), noted that she was "terrified" of telling people she wrote young adult fiction, even her husband.

None of these examples just happened. They were the result of careful thought and preparation to add more pizazz to SDCC. Use these examples to help you and your panel moderator brainstorm all the possibilities.

SOLVING THE PROGRAMMATIC PUNCH

Here's the challenge: A full day of panels discussing Programmatic Trading covering intense topics such as blockchain, compensation for ad fraud, and other detailed discussions has the potential to put people to sleep.

This is the perfect time to add more pizazz to your panel!

Enter Lynn Lester, a Scottish dynamo with a sense for drama and daring. As Managing Director of Live Events for *The Drum*, a global media company, she hosts *Programmatic Punch* events all over the world. But for this first-time event in New York City, she needed to go big and make sure this event was a home run. Here's the promotional copy which she infused with boxing metaphors:

What is Programmatic Punch?
As a famous boxer once said 'Everyone has a plan until they get a punch in the face.' Well, a combination of innovation and regulation in ad-tech could—metaphorically speaking—add up to such a punch. The Drum's Programmatic Punch is designed to help you duck and dive to ensure you exploit the opportunities of this new age, as opposed to succumbing to its threats. The event aims to serve as a wake-up call about the revolution this industry is going through.

Now that doesn't sound boring at all!

As Lester was planning out the day, she focused on how the audience should feel. The Drum brand is known for its energy and fun, so she focused on how she could make the event fun and energizing even though they were debating dry, serious topics.

So she brainstormed everything about boxing and asked, "How can we make this work?"
- As you walk in, you are greeted with posters of boxing matches showing the topics and panelists.
- At the far end of the room, you see a boxing ring (yep, that's right!) with chairs on three sides of the ring.
- The lighting is dark with spotlights showcasing the posters and ring.
- Loud fight music is playing (think Survivor's *Eye of the Tiger* and Black Eyed Peas *Pump It*)

You instantly knew this wasn't going to be a boring corporate panel.

Just minutes before the fight was to begin (*ahem*, the event was to begin), the referee (aka emcee) stepped into the ring while a microphone dropped down from the ceiling. Lester immediately got participation with a quiz about Scottish terms related to boxing. The prize? A bottle of whiskey. (At 9am, no less!)

Then the Voice of God announced the first fight: "Welcome to the ring, and from the red corner..." and the moderator and speakers would come out of their corners fighting. Some even wore boxing gloves! Simultaneously, a sign man walked around the ring with a big sign that clearly indicated this was Round One. When the panel was ready to begin, a bell sounded. And when it was over, the bell signaled the end of Round One! Short break, and then they were on to Round Two!

At the end of the day, The Drum offered Scottish treats and a dram of whiskey—after all, the company was founded in Glasgow!

How creative and exciting! So you might be wondering:

- How much did the speakers know about this? Lester says they didn't know much. They knew that they were going to be in a boxing ring on high chairs. And they were encouraged to use words related to boxing. But since this was a first time thing, Lester was sensitive to not push the envelope too far. When I mentioned the idea of having the panelists come out in bathrobes, she said, "Yes, we thought of that, but thought that might be too gimmicky for our first time. We hadn't met many of these people before and we didn't want to make them feel uncomfortable."

- What about safety? How did the panelists get into the ring? Lester was very attentive to the health and safety of all in the room. So there were stairs on each side of the ring and people to pull the ropes up and to help the panelists enter the ring.

- How many people were there? Around 200 with people flowing in and out throughout the day. The biggest surprise was that "tons of people stayed to talk" which is always a positive sign of hosting a great day.

- The key to success? Lester said that she brainstormed all the possibilities using the boxing theme and wove it into the marketing materials. And then took the physical elements (five senses) and asked, "How can I make that work? What will wow my audience? Create curiosity and fun?"

She did a masterful job of creating lively and informative panel discussions with an otherwise dry topic.

Bravo Lynn Lester and The Drum!

CHAPTER TWO
DESIGN AN INSPIRING PANEL

Be audience-centric when making decisions about your format. Think about their
education and engagement needs and design a creative panel experience that will
deliver a transformational learning experience that they can't stop talking about.
~ Sarah Michel

THE MAJORITY OF PANELS rely on the same four formats with up to five segments:

- **MAIN STAGE STYLE.** Hard-hitting, short panel discussion with the keynote/main stage presenters with no audience Q&A.

- **Q&A STYLE.** Ample opportunity to solicit questions from the audience. A 2–5 minute introduction of the topic and panelists, 25 minutes of curated questions from the moderator, 25 minutes of audience questions ending with a summary and thanks.

- **INITIAL REMARKS STYLE.** Panelists tee up their unique perspectives on the topic. A 2–5 minute introduction of the topic with each panelist taking 5 minutes to introduce themselves and their perspectives on the topic. Then 20 minutes of curated questions from the moderator, 10–15 minutes of Q&A with the audience ending with a summary and thanks.

- **PRESENTATION STYLE.** Panelists need to do an in-depth sharing of the topic in order to bring the audience up to speed. A 2–5 minute introduction of the topic and panelists. Each panelist has 10–15 minutes of uninterrupted sharing of their perspectives, 5–10 minutes of Q&A ending with a summary and thanks.[2]

This chapter will give you some ideas beyond these traditional boring formats. While these four traditional styles all work, the key is to select or create a panel format that resonates with *your* audience and is congruent with the topic. As the panel moderator, it's your job to add the pizazz!

---

[2] I am least fond of the Presentation Style Format. Remember, "to rise and make a speech...is the one unforgivable offense." So don't offend your audience. Do NOT let your panelists give a speech during the discussion. If your panelists are going to give a presentation, give them a slot on the program for their presentations, THEN start the panel discussion.

1 CREATE AN INTRIGUING TITLE

The title of your panel discussion is the first opportunity to capture your audience's attention. *Panel Discussion: The Future of the Industry* is rarely an attention-grabbing headline. In fact, anything with Panel Discussion causes the eye to glance over the explanation. So don't do it.

An intriguing title signals your intent to be lively and engaging instead of dull and boring. A catchy and effective title should:

- Be appropriate to the occasion or tie into the conference theme.
- Provide enough information about the subject so potential attendees can tell whether this is likely to be of interest to them.
- Be succinct and to the point.
- Pique the interest of the potential audience.

Perhaps you're like me. I acknowledge that I need a lively title, yet I can't always think of one. So I look at magazine titles for inspiration. Magazine editors have been attracting readers for years; browse your magazine rack for ideas. If you're going to follow a television show format, then take a riff off the title of the show. For example, *Real Time with Kristin Arnold,* or *American Idol* (substitute Idol for the primary profession in the audience). My all-time favorite is *Inside the Actor's Studio* (substitute Actor for the primary profession in your audience).

CEO of the Intrigue Agency, Sam Horn is renowned for helping individuals and organizations create intriguing ideas and original approaches that help them break out versus blend in. In her book, *POP! Create the Perfect Pitch, Title and Tagline for Anything!* [Perigee-Penguin, 2009], she suggests you identify your Points of Distinction (PODs):

- What is a common truth about your topic? Don't bore people by featuring that in your title or description. Saying the same thing as everyone else is a prescription for blending in.
- How can you say the opposite instead of the obvious? A panel discussion entitled The Customer is NOT Always Right that delves into how employees can deal with chronic complainers who consistently break the rules is likely to elicit interest. Many people would welcome what promises to be a tell-it-like-it-is discussion that addresses a real problem without a Pollyanna approach.
- Make the topic itself controversial or even polarizing. Nutritional Standards for Centenarians at Independent Living Facilities might be too vague to pique the audience's interest—unless you are a geriatric nutritionist desperate for continuing education credits! How else might we create interest in a topic? My brain starts going toward something like:
  - Breakthroughs or Breakups: The latest thinking in nutritional standards for 100$^+$ year olds. (The caveat here is that there IS some latest thinking going on.)
  - Fact or Fiction: Myths that Perpetuate Nutritional Standards at Independent Living Facilities Today.
  - Should Centenarians Eat This or That?

The key is to hint at controversy in the title and/or the short write-up of the panel discussion.

RIFF A TV SHOW 2

You don't have to rely on the four traditional panel formats. Instead, add a little pizazz with a more entertaining and engaging format—and the best source of inspiration comes from television.

That's right. Television.

Popular television shows are great venues to look for ways to add pizazz to your panel. It can be something as simple as riffing a well-known game show, mimicking a talk show or doing a takeoff on a news commentary.

Remember Phil Donahue? (I know. I'm showing my age.) He pioneered walking into the audience and reflecting the questions and conversation to the guests (panelists) on the stage. That's called Donahue Style—although more recently, people call it Oprah Style.

What about John McLaughlin, host of *the McLaughlin Group*? John has a loud and powerful voice. He often makes witty and sometimes arguably outlandish predictions. Usually, John sets the context for the topic and may take a poll from the audience. The conversation starts out mild enough. As opposing viewpoints emerge, there is more verbal sparring, good-natured ribbing, and loud crosstalk as panelists attempt to out-yell the others.

I grew up on *60 Minutes* and their version of Point/Counterpoint where the topic is presented and each panelist presents their side which is then rebutted by another panelist.

Or take inspiration from *American Idol, The Voice,* or other reality TV contests where audience members ask for feedback from the expert panelists.

Or tone it down into a chatty, conversational style. Think *Friends* at the Central Perk Coffee Shop. It's an intimate conversation where the audience is privy to the thinking of the panelists.

There are so many other TV show formats that you could imitate. The possibilities are endless.

HOW TO ADAPT A TV SHOW TO YOUR PANEL

STEP 1   **CHOOSE A PROGRAM**
Identify a program that you think your audience will identify with AND has the right blend of interaction. Some examples I've seen are David Letterman, Jimmy Fallon, The View, The Ellen DeGeneres Show, Crossfire, Real Time with Bill Maher, Inside the Actor's Studio, The Wendy Williams Show, So You Think You Can Dance?, American Idol, and Friends.

STEP 2   **BRAINSTORM ELEMENTS**
Brainstorm all the different elements of the program: the format, the staging, the guests, the conversational style, the interactions with guests and audience. Let's take The Tonight Show Starring Jimmy Fallon show as an example. He has several bits in his show:

- *Pros & Cons.* Fallon weighs the positives and the negatives on a particular topic of current events, with the Pro setting up the punch line, in the form of the Con.
- *Tonight Show Suggestion Box.* Fallon responds to written suggestions, purportedly submitted by audience members, about ways to improve the show. As a result, the segment usually features three or four unrelated short comedy bits.

- *Tonight Show Hashtags.* Fallon puts out a call on Twitter each Wednesday for actual viewers to submit funny or absurd tweets based around a particular hashtag topic. Fallon then reads a few of the most comedic responses on Thursday's show.

- *Thank You Notes.* Fallon writes weekly thank you notes to people in the news, current events, inanimate objects, and other random subjects to comedic effect. Each note is accompanied by reflective piano music from The Roots' James Poyser, and usually results in a hilarious exchange between Fallon and Higgins.

- *Superlatives.* Fallon shows photos of athletes and gives them captions styled like those that might be used in a high school yearbook.

- *Screen Grabs.* Viewers submit actual screen shots from various media (phones, internet, television) that contain typos or similar errors with humorous results.

- *Do Not Read List.* Jimmy shares real published books found in actual libraries that have awkward titles or subject matter, an ironic author's name, or other humorous element.

- *Ew!* Jimmy portrays a teenage girl named Sara and invites many celebrities to be in his basement. Through the sketch, all girls say "Ew!" a lot!

And he does it all behind a wooden desk with one guest coming out at a time. He's wearing a suit and there is a band playing between breaks.

STEP 3   **BRAINSTORM IDEAS**
Brainstorm all the potential ways you could infuse that same kind of look and feel into your program. Don't worry whether they are any good at this stage, either. Just have fun with a few folks on the program committee and brainstorm the possibilities. For example:

- The moderator can come out and do a monologue like Jimmy, wearing a similar suit.

- The moderator can do a Pro & Con about the topic—making it funny and relevant.

- Who might be an unusual guest? One that is on the periphery of the topic but still applicable and can add value to the conversation? Or, can you have someone portray a luminary in the topic that you couldn't possibly afford to come to your meeting?

STEP 4   **NARROW THE LIST**
Now go through your list from Step 3 to see if any might have some real-world potential. (This is entirely up to you, the moderator, and the program team. You can even get the panelists involved if they have already been selected.)

STEP 5   **CREATE THE TITLE**
Think of a clever title that includes part of the show's name, but also the title of the organization, the topic, the meeting theme or other significant words. For example, a sales conference mimicked The Ellen DeGeneres Show and called the program The Sellin' DeGeneres Show. I am often asked to moderate the deconstruction of a presentation at the professional speakers' associations and I call it Inside the Speaker's Studio.

STEP 6   **HAVE FUN!**
Have fun putting this together. Not only will you have fun, but the audience will too!

Obviously, TV formats work well in the virtual world. Pay particular attention to the visual aspects of a TV show and see how well you can replicate it.

THE HOT SEAT FORMAT 3

Think of the television show *American Idol* where the panelists are expert judges and contestants are receiving real-time feedback from the audience. Or the show *Shark Tank* where the panelists are venture capitalists and the participants are entrepreneurs seeking funding.

The key here is to have subject matter experts as panelists and audience members who desperately want real-time, live feedback on their idea, question, issue, product, or thingamajig.

The voyeuristic joy of this format is that it is completely Unplugged. Unscripted. Unrehearsed. Which can drive some meeting organizers crazy, but audiences love it and learn vicariously through the process.

By the way, it's best to preselect those who will sit on the hot seat for two reasons:

1. You want to make sure the idea, product or service is relevant and universal to most, if not all, of the audience.

2. Make sure the person on the hot seat really wants feedback. Sometimes, it's hard to hear your baby is ugly!

Here's one type of format you can use:

0:00   Welcome, Format Overview, Agenda and Ground Rules

0:02   Brief Introduction of All the Panelists

0:05   Contestant #1
- Moderator introduces the contestant and the issue he/she wants resolved/feedback
- Contestant provides background/context, relevant information
- Panelists/audience provide feedback
- Moderator summarizes/checks in with contestant

0:22   Contestant #2
- Follow the same format and timing for the second and third Contestants

0:39   Contestant #3
- Follow the same format and timing for the second and third Contestants

0:56   Summarize

0:58   Thank you/administrative directions

1:00   Adjourn

4 FRIENDS CAFÉ STYLE FORMAT

I might be dating myself here, but think of the television show *Friends*. There are NO formal introductions. Characters (aka panelists) simply walk on the stage set with comfortable, café style furniture and strike up conversation about a topic that the audience is absolutely fascinated to overhear.

To run a Café Style Panel, the moderator, who might be cast as the barista, and Panelist #1 walk onto the stage already engaged in a conversation. In the first few sentences of this impromptu discussion, they are setting the context for why this is important to discuss.

A few seconds later, Panelist #2 walks on and joins the discussion, then Panelist #3 joins in, and finally Panelist #4 completes the panel.

Since you won't have any formal introductions, you may want to use some slides to introduce the moderator and each panelist as they walk onto the stage.

The moderator/barista then expertly facilitates a lively conversation among the panelists.

With just a few minutes to go, panelists summarize what their key takeaways are and then panelists and moderator exit the stage in the same random fashion they entered.

And the audience applause? Oddly enough, it starts while the last panelist leaves the stage.

> This works best if the panelists are physically in the same room and the audience feels like they have dropped into an intimate discussion.

PITCH PANEL FORMAT 5

In today's innovation-driven environment, everyone from executives to event organizers can appreciate novel ways of moving ideas closer to impact. From external sites like Kickstarter to internal idea marketplaces where employees can upvote their favorites, there are myriad ways of evaluating fresh ideas.

What if you want to deeply explore only a few ideas, in a way that idea authors can interact with a panel of experts? You might want to consider a Pitch Panel where creators offer their ideas to a panel of experts. In return, the experts offer advice and perhaps a prize. The TV shows *Shark Tank* or *Dragon's Den* are popular examples of a Pitch Panel.

Unlike many panels, there are quite a few moving parts to this type of format, so I asked Raoul Encinas, co-founder of CoMotiv and event organizer for PHX Street Pitch, to help identify key components.

OBJECTIVES. Why are you having this Pitch Panel? What are the objectives? In our case, our intention was to bring more attention to Arizona Early Stage Start Up companies, while also building up the public speaking skills of Arizona-based founders.

FORMAT. This is the tricky part and you really need to think this through. In our case, we decided:

- *Emcee.* To have an emcee (a bit of a different role from moderator) kick off the event, provide end-to-end continuity for the event, and handle closing announcements.

- *Timeframe.* Each pitcher was given exactly five minutes to present their idea. Some Pitch Panels leave it up to the pitcher to decide (like *Shark Tank*). Others will give them a slide deck template to follow. We decided to do something a bit different, leveraging the ignite style talk format: We gave them 20 slides of their choosing where the slides would advance every 15 seconds, automatically. This forced the pitchers to get creative plus we knew we would stay on time.

- *Q&A.* Obviously, there are going to be some questions—either from the panelists, the audience or both. We decided to limit questioning to our expert panel, but I really love the idea of crowdsourcing questions from the audience.

- *On-the-Spot Feedback.* Decide when and how the panelists will give feedback. For our event, we shared feedback shortly after the event and many of the pitchers were complimented or coached on:

  - Clarity of message.
  - Their personal story: why their idea was important to them and necessary to bring forth into the world.
  - Explanation of the business case and projections.
  - Call to action and how they will use the prize (money).

DELIBERATIONS. Determine how the winner(s) will be determined (if there even is one).

- If the panel judges the winner, will they do that in full view of the audience? Will they adjourn to deliberate in private? Make sure the panelists know the deliberations process to decide the winner. In our case, we had a facilitator manage the process and keep them on time.

- If the audience judges the winner, you can go by the loudest cheers or take a vote using crowdsourcing technology.

- Encinas says, "Energy escapes the room when the judges leave the room." If there is going to be lag time between the last pitch and the announcement of the winner, then you want to fill that with something interesting and entertaining. We filled the time with three high schooler entrepreneurs sharing their start up story (not pitching), using the same Ignite-style format as the main pitchers.

DATE AND LOCATION. Select a date and location that aligns with your objectives. We wanted lots of visibility for early stage startups, so we held this in conjunction with Phoenix Startup Week and Small Business Appreciation Day. We also held this on a main street in downtown Phoenix (ergo the name, Street Pitch.) We literally closed down the street, brought in furniture, carpeting, and staging to make it special.

PITCHERS. You'll receive far more applications than you will have room (or time) to include. Identify ahead of time just how many applications you will approve. We decided on ten pitches at five minutes each. That's almost an hour – not including the front and back end of the panel. Any more would have been too long.

APPLICATION PROCESS. Determine the criteria you will use to narrow down the field. How will you inform those who were selected as well as those who weren't? Are you going to provide any feedback (or not)?

PANELISTS. Decide and invite who will be the experts listening to the pitches, asking questions and judging the winner(s). "Keep in mind, as VIP stakeholders, they don't have an appetite to come early just to sit around," says Encinas. "Plan for a dedicated host who can keep them engaged from the moment they arrive." You'll need to communicate the logistics, evaluation criteria and process clearly. We had three panelists determine the winner and the first runner-up.

PRIZE. If there is a winner, determine the prize to be won, and make sure you understand the legal implications of this. We had applicants sign a waiver as a condition of participating in the process. Legal disclaimer: Consult your attorney for compliance to rules and regulations when raising money.

COACHING. Since many of our early start-up pitchers were fairly young and relatively inexperienced when it came to pitching their idea (especially using a five minute *Ignite* process), we mandated a two-hour Speaker Bootcamp as well as optional personal coaching. (I coached three of the pitchers through the gauntlet.)

Pitch panels are a tremendous amount of work to organize, yet a ton of fun to watch creative minds at work.

THE CASE STUDY FORMAT 6

Detailed stories that are based on an intensive analysis of a person or a community within a given environment are called case studies. Especially in academic settings, presenters often just present a case study (which can get downright boring), so let's add more pizazz by engaging the audience.

- First, select an appropriate case study for your topic. You can cite your own hard-learned scenarios or purchase them from management review journals. Harvard Business School, for example, is famous for publishing case studies wherein a problem situation is outlined and various experts weigh in on what should be done. *Note: If you are going to create your own case studies, remove all explicit or indirect references to the parties involved that could lead to the identification of the organization or individual.*

- Select panelists who were either part of the case study or can comment on the case study. Make sure there are diverse points of view represented.

- At the beginning of the panel discussion, tee up the case study as a problem to be solved. Describe the starting assumptions and provide as much detail as needed for the audience to be able to discuss the issue. If the situation is complex, you may want to provide a one page handout or project a slide with the pertinent information.

- Ask the audience to break into small groups to identify problems. Give them a few minutes to discuss.

- If time allows, debrief answers from the audience or ask them to submit their answers into a polling app. (I use Slido.com for this.) If you don't have time, go straight to the panelists to discuss the main problems.

- When ready, move into the solution space where the panelists share a handful of potential solutions.

- Let the participants discuss the advantages and disadvantages of each alternative. If time allows, debrief answers from the audience. If you don't have time, go straight to the panelists to discuss advantages and disadvantages.

- Then, share what actually happened.

- If time allows, ask the audience to discuss the relevance of the case study to their own current reality. What lessons did they learn? Key take-aways? Debrief a few answers from the audience and you've finished a lively and informative case study panel discussion.

Use the breakout group function to allow participants to discuss the case study. Ask the small groups to identify a spokesperson to ensure the debrief is short and orderly.

7 RAPID-FIRE FORMAT

Rapid-fire panel discussion sounds much sexier than a boring panel discussion, doesn't it? I admit, I was intrigued with the title when I first stumbled upon Colorado Real Estate Investor's Association's *90 Questions in 90 Minutes: Legal Rapid Fire Panel.* That's gotta be a tough one to moderate since most lawyers can't answer a question in less than a minute!

There are many different varieties of rapid-fire panels; this is my version where the audience asks the questions in a fast-paced Q&A:

- Moderator welcome includes the format overview, agenda, and ground rules.
- Panelist introductions with a 30 second introductory comment from each panelist, stating their diverse and specific viewpoint on the topic.
- Audience Q&A (the rapid fire part) as audience members queue up to ask their questions either behind a microphone stand or using a throwable microphone.
- Each audience member states the question in one or two sentences. The moderator quickly intervenes if the questioner takes longer.
- One of the panelists answers the question with a specified period of time (perhaps 45 seconds; depends on the topic).
- Keep going until you have only 5 minutes to the end.
- Moderator summarizes and asks panelists to quickly (state the timeframe such as 15 seconds) offer one key point for the audience to remember.
- Moderator mentions any administrative items, next event on the program and thanks all for their rapt participation.

You can use a buzzer, or game-show music to keep it moving and add a bit of levity. You can even have each of the panelists stand behind a lectern for the entire session (think Presidential debates).

> Think through how to get questions *quickly* and who is going to pose them.
> Perhaps you've gathered many questions prior to the panel from
> social media or you have a vibrant social media stream.
> You can also use a meeting app to get your questions.

THE SME FORMAT 8

Event producer Hugh Lee created the SME Format while producing the DigitalNow event. Lee kept calling the panelists SMEs (Subject Matter Experts) since they didn't fall into traditional panelist roles.

So let's follow the process as described by Hugh:

- Keynote speaker for 35–40 minutes on raised stage in a semi-theater in the round (three groupings around the stage).
- The keynote speaker steps down into the middle of the room OR stays on the stage, depending on which works best for the room set-up.
- Four panelists/SMEs are seated in director chairs on a platform at the four corners of the room. They interview the speaker using questions curated with the sponsor, the production company, or the moderator. *Note: Even though the SMEs are selected because of their topic expertise, they are more like hard-hitting reporters who ask pointed questions (think Anderson Cooper or Martha McCallum).*
- The moderator works the room ensuring the conversation flows from four sources:
  1. SMEs ask questions.
  2. Audience members ask questions from standing microphones placed strategically in the room.
  3. Audience questions are sent to the moderator from the meeting app.
  4. Moderator asks follow up questions. The moderator may even take a poll (or more) on a key point using a meeting app or a simple show of hands.
- Moderator summarizes the conversation, asks for a short closing remark from the keynoter and we're done!

9 THE ILLUSTRATED PANEL FORMAT

In the book *TED Talks: The Official TED Guide to Public Speaking*, author Chris Anderson describes the Illustrated Interview as a visual format that encourages some preparation by both interviewer and interviewee. For our purposes, we're going to expand that to multiple interviewees which makes it a panel, not an interview.

I'll let Anderson describe it for you:

"It's a conversation accompanied by a sequence of images [or video] that has been worked out in advance by both parties. The images act as chapter markers for the various topics to be covered, and they add refreshing reference points for the conversation." Chris also adds, "It allows interviewees to really think about how they want to structure an idea that matters to them. And it decreases the risk of rambling or getting bogged down...[the interviewer] has the option to query any points that aren't clear, live on stage, while the talk is in progress."

Yes, orchestrating this with one person can be a challenge. Doing it with three or four panelists can be downright daunting. Can it be done? Yes! Especially if you're talking about something quite visual or auditory.

As the moderator, you *may* give the panelists the option to have one or two slides if needed to illustrate a specific point they want to make. Load all slides into one slide deck so you can be in control of which slide is presented (if any).

It's a flow between one topic and another as well as a delicate balance between preparation and spontaneity. Are you up for the challenge?

Have the slides ready to be shared onscreen.

THE UNPANEL FORMAT 10

I've seen several panels declare themselves an UnPanel—a panel without a moderator. And it always ends up with one of the panelists serving as the *de facto* moderator. After all, how do you keep a handful of people focused?

In fact, several years ago, I witnessed such a panel at the National Speakers Association. Five well-known speakers decided to have a live, unplugged conversation for an hour. It really wasn't going anywhere until Randy Pennington started exerting a little rudder control over the conversation. Thank goodness—although it reaffirmed my belief that a panel really needs a moderator!

Fast forward to last month where I watched Randy and two others from that earlier panel (Scott McKain and Larry Winget) on another panel, but this time, it was truly a panel without a moderator. It was informative, fun and a seamless conversation where each panelist had equal time and was equally respectful. So I called Randy to find out the difference between the two UnPanels, here is what he said:

LIMIT TO THREE PEOPLE. It's easier to have an UnPanel with only three people, five was too many for everyone to insert their ideas in a short period of time without a moderator.

HIGH DEGREE OF FAMILIARITY. Although they are all good friends, a high degree of collegiality didn't guarantee a successful outcome. However, they had done several programs and panels together, so they understood each other's strengths, styles, and content. They knew the rhythm of starting and stopping, interjecting and withdrawing, so it became a fluid dance between the panelists.

DESIGNATE ROLES TO PLAY. Just like any good reality TV show, panelists need to know their roles. In this case, Larry's the "provocateur," Scott's the "high concept" guy, and Randy claimed the "make it work" title. They all switched roles as needed, but knowing the basics provided structure.

HAVE A STRATEGY AND STRUCTURE. The three of them met the night before to talk about the key points they wanted to drive home and how they were going to proceed through the session. In this case, they had a handout to use as a backup plan just in case audience questions didn't cover their key points. They also confabbed out in the hall right before the session started to weave any in the moment tie-ins they wanted to emphasize.

EBB AND FLOW. They resisted thinking about this as a traditional panel. Even though there were three chairs positioned on a stage at the front of the room, I don't think I saw all of them sit down at the same time. There was usually one person center stage speaking with the others in the wings. Then that speaker would turn it over or someone would walk up and the other would recede to the side. Because of that familiarity with each other, they were able to understand intuitively when they needed to move on or balance their airtime.

An UnPanel discussion, while not impossible, does require a certain amount of chemistry and respect between panelists. And if you use this format, I hope you stay friends!

> This format is hard to pull off in the real world, and even harder in the virtual world. If you have a tight-knit group of panelists, you could challenge them to see how they might structure a virtual UnPanel.

11   PEER-BASED IMPROMPTU FORMAT

Event planner Matt Dadey shared this innovative panel format he experienced at the World Education Congress. They had three panels that occurred throughout the one-hour session—with *no* pre-selected panelists. Matt explained, "None of it was preplanned which is pretty much a planner's dream come true! Locking down and prepping panelists is one of the reasons I personally get stressed out when I think about panels."

Obviously, the moderator put some thought into the design of the panels, but it's a pretty simple process to follow (as described by Matt):

Once the session starts:

1.   Moderator asks a starter question such as, "Rate yourself on a scale of 'one' to 'ten' of your knowledge on contract negotiations. Use the left wall for 'one' and the right wall for '10' as the scale."

2.   The participants get up and stand where they think they would rate their knowledge on that topic.

3.   The moderator then selects three people who have the most knowledge on that topic from the 10 area. These three experts then make up the first panel. The audience asks questions and those panelists give insight.

The second panel repeats the process, but with a harder topic because now people know what's going on. The moderator will probably have to pick from the 7 to 8 range since the audience will naturally shift left a bit in fear of being on a panel. That's okay though. The point of this activity is primarily to encourage peer discussion.

The third panel goes the same way in format, but Matt's idea is to flip the script. For this panel, the moderator would pull from the left wall and have them ask questions to the audience about what they want to know more about on the topic. This helps bring people out of their shell who otherwise wouldn't be as engaged, and helps them get questions answered that they might have been too scared to ask.

As Matt explains, "This is definitely different than a traditional panel, since you cannot guarantee the people who think they are experts are actually experts, but it keeps people engaged by making them move around for the scale exercise and when the panel is made up of their peers they seem to be more likely to ask questions and encourage discussion. I know that I don't typically ask questions in a panel if the panelists are all CEOs because it's intimidating, but this format eliminates that and encourages peers teaching peers."

> In the digital world, you aren't going to be able to line people up in a room. However, you can post a continuum on the screen and ask the participants to annotate an arrow as to where they fall on that continuum. Typically, the program will default having their name on the arrow so you can call them out by name.

THE P³ (P-CUBED) FORMAT 12

I attended a national convention that used an innovative format that included a panel discussion. I'll call it the P³ Format. Here's how it went:

PRESENTATION. An intriguing, provocative speaker shares ideas and wisdom for 30–40 minutes. (BTW, if you are wondering if your speaker is intriguing or provocative, the answer is probably NO. Find another speaker.)

PANEL. Bring on a panel of three to four D.E.E.P. (they are **d**iverse, **e**xperts, **e**loquent, and **p**repared) panelists to discuss the impact of the speaker's presentation and topic for 20–30 minutes. (No audience Q&A included.)

PONDER. Have the audience share their reactions/application of the information within a smaller group for 15 minutes.

See? That's three Ps in a row. It can be quite engaging and interesting.

> *Use the breakout group function to allow participants to share their reactions/application of the information.*

13 AUDIENCE DRIVEN FORMAT

Sometimes, you just need to let the audience drive the conversation. It really has to be a perfect storm of conditions:

1. The audience is familiar with the topic and has lots of questions they want to ask the expert panelists.
2. The audience is already familiar with the panelists—either they were introduced to them earlier in the program or they are well-known in that community.
3. The audience size is manageable; for example, fewer than 300 people.
4. The session is less than 60 minutes.
5. You want to maximize value for the audience.

When all five conditions occur, dispense with the introductory rigmarole and get down to business quickly.

Spend just a few minutes to introduce the topic and the objectives while you are inviting the panelists to join you on stage.

You'll want to emphasize that this discussion is going to be driven by the *audience*. That you and will facilitate the conversation based on the questions the audience asks.

Share the directions on how you are going to solicit questions from the audience:

- **LIVE.** Take questions from the floor via a queue, runners, or by the moderator roaming the crowd.
- **SCREENED.** Filter and prioritize the questions via question cards, texts, tweets, or by small groups chatting and popping up with their best questions.
- **CROWDSOURCED.** Use a meeting app such as Slido.com so the audience can create and like the questions.
- **SEEDED.** It's a bit of a risky strategy, so you can also ask trusted audience members to ask a straightforward or supplied question.

Then take the first question, the question you see most often in the cards, texts, tweets, or the top-voted question. Let a panelist respond while encouraging comments that add to the conversation.

Then take the next question, and then the next, until you have about five minutes left.

With just a few minutes at the end of the session, wrap it up very quickly with a summarizing statement and then ask each panelist, "What's the one thing you thought you were going to be asked, but you weren't? And what's your answer?"

Thank the panelists and audience for their contributions, the sponsor for their support, and send them off to the next activity.

FISHBOWL FORMAT 14

While theater-in-the-round is a unique audience-centered seating arrangement (gaining more popularity), it is all the more challenging in which to have a robust panel discussion.

The most prevalent is the fishbowl format where panelists sit in a circle on the center stage and the audience sits around the stage. In this format, the audience is listening in on the café-style conversation among panelists. While this format fosters a much more intimate discussion, the audience will always see the back of at least one panelist. Furthermore, it becomes more problematic to engage the audience in a typical Q&A.

See Tip #40—Panel-in-the-Round for more details on how to set up a fishbowl format.

Because the fishbowl format is about the physical placement of the panelists and audience, this cannot be done in the virtual environment. However, it can be done well in the hybrid version—just use the virtual audience as an outer ring.

15 MUSICAL CHAIR GAME FORMAT

Remember the game Musical Chairs? It's a party game where you have one less chair than the number of people. When the music starts, everyone circles the chairs. When the music stops, everyone scrambles for a chair. Obviously, one person is left standing, and they are out of the game. You keep doing this until there is one person left.

So what does this have to do with a panel? My fellow panel moderator, Elizabeth Marshall, was told to use this format for a panel discussion. You see, the meeting organizer asked seven people to participate (which is about three or four people too many) AND the panel was being held late in the day. So, in order to add a little pizzazz, they wanted to do musical chairs. Only for this panel, they would just keep three chairs on the stage and panelists had to fight for the right to sit in a chair.

Okay, maybe I'm embellishing here. They didn't fight like Mad Max, but they did have to sit in a chair if they wanted to speak.

Marshall said, "This was one of the most challenging panel formats I've ever had because the structure was suggested to me by the organization. I had to think about a lot of different things. What types of questions could I ask in a two, three or even five-minute stretch before we got up to do musical chairs, and then I wouldn't even know who would be sitting down. While I could prepare for all seven panelists that would be on the stage with us, I didn't know ahead of time what mix of three would be in front of me. I had to think in real time about the topics and questions and directions we could take it. I could continue the conversation from the previous segment but in looking at the three people in a split second I might say no we're going to segue [to another topic]. It really challenged me to work with both my *preparation* and *structure* as well as really listening and watching for what in the moment would work the best given our overall goal and conversation. It was wild but fun!"

So here's how Marshall conducted the musical chairs format: "I introduced all seven panelists to start and set the context. We had the first three sit down so that wasn't chaos. I picked them ahead of time (or they drew straws) and then we had the first five minutes of curated Q&A. Then the A/V guy turned on the music and all the panelists were circling around and three new people sat in the chairs. I also gave them some instruction on 'Don't be the person that sits down every single time. You know we need to have some diversity!'"

Marshall summarized, "Despite the challenges of this format, I was able to curate a cohesive discussion that was both entertaining and of value to the audience."

Connect audio input from your computer into your platform
(vs. playing music over your voice audio connection).

Play the music and turn off participants' audio and visual.
Select three participants and turn their audio/video on.
They are now in the chairs.

Keep the other participants muted.

EMPTY CHAIR FORMAT 16

The Empty Chair format is perfect for when you want to encourage deep dialogue that extends out into the audience.

Simply add one extra chair for your panel. So if you have confirmed three panelists, set the stage for four panelists.

The empty seat is for an audience member who has a strong point of view to add to the conversation. During the introductory remarks, invite the audience to come and sit in the seat if they have something constructive and of value to add to the conversation. Once that person has contributed, ask them to go back to their seat to let the next point of view emerge from the audience. OR another audience member puts a hand on the shoulder of the person occupying the empty seat. That's the signal to finish their thought and move along.

A more daring format is the **musical chairs format** where an audience member can tap *any* panelist on the shoulder and replace that panelist in the chair.

Use the Raised Hand feature to call on a person who has a strong point of view to add to the conversation.

Call out the name of the person, unmute them and spotlight that person as the person in the empty chair. The moderator continues to invite people to "take a chair" and take people off the spotlight.

17 LAYERED GROUP LISTENING FORMAT

Panel moderator Chip Bell shared a unique format he's used at Harley Davidson, Victoria's Secret and other companies. He calls it Layered Group Listening which works with no more than 50 people in a room.

Here's how Bell describes it:

- Start with a panel with five or six customers seated in a circle. Outside that circle, create a second circle with the people who serve customers or people like them. Create an outer third circle with the leaders and managers of the organization.

- Moderate a conversation with the customers in the first circle. The second circle can ask questions of the first circle for clarification. The people on the outer circle can't say anything—which is really hard. Bell also shared that "when we did this for Harley Davidson, the people on the outside ring got fined a hundred bucks if they opened their mouths because leaders always want to say something. You can also give the people in the outer circle the opportunity to send the moderator a card to 'Ask them this…' so that they could interject their questions."

- Then, the customers leave and the front line people in the second circle move center circle where the customers were. The leaders and managers in the outer ring move in to the second (middle) circle.

- Moderate a second panel discussion with the frontline people reacting to what they heard. The leaders in the second circle can only ask questions for clarification.

- The moderator can finish the session with a problem solving discussion to summarize what was said and what the organization is going to do about it.

- When Bell did this final session with Victoria's Secret, they brought the customers back to participate in the problem solving with everybody in the room. But that depends on what kind of dirty linen got aired in the process. Sometimes you bring the customers back, and sometimes you don't. Depends on the organization and what they want.

The fact that you're trying to listen through layers brings awareness and learning to the organization. Sometimes you might have frontline people who say, "I don't want my boss hearing about something I might have done, or someone like me might have done." That's what I used to think. Actually, what we get instead is, "Thank goodness they were in here and got to hear the same thing I've been complaining about or fussing about or struggling with. And they got to hear it first hand from a customer. Then they involved me in problem solving and how we deal with it."

Of course, you can't set everyone up in a circle, but you can orchestrate the movement of people in and out of the virtual meeting room, and controlling their audio. Try color coordinating their outfits or backgrounds as a way to group them.

ASK A FILL-IN-THE-BLANK FORMAT 18

You may not use this panel discussion format very often, but when you want the audience to walk a mile in another person's shoes, try the Ask a <u>Fill-in-the-Blank</u> format.

As reported by the Star Tribune (paraphrased): It was after the July 2016 shooting of Philando Castile by a St. Anthony police officer. Roseville resident Nyia Harris wanted her community to hear the perspective of black men regarding policing, bias, and everyday life. So she went to Do Good Roseville and pitched Ask a Black Man during a February panel discussion and Q&A session that ended with a standing ovation by an audience of 100 people. "I wanted black male voices to be out there," said Harris, a mother of two and a part-time teaching assistant at her children's school. "But I was going to be one and done."

Ahhh...not so fast, Mrs. Harris. Your idea has taken fire!

The enthusiastic response by the public that night, and a continued hunger for honest conversation, has instead fueled continuing conversations that show no signs of abating. Ask a Black Man led to Ask a Black Man-Part Two which included three white men on the panel. That led to Ask a Muslim Woman, Ask a Community Youth and Ask a Veteran. In 2018, planned panels include Ask A Dreamer, Ask A Muslim Woman-Part Two, Ask an Adoptive Parent and Ask a LGBTQIA (Lesbian, Gay, Bisexual, Transgender, Queer, Intersex, Asexual).

So how does this work? The moderator solicits questions from the audience, typically using 3"x5" note cards, but you can also use crowdsourcing technology (especially if people want anonymity). The moderator explains the process, sets some ground rules, and starts the Q&A session. Harris says, "All I ask is that the people be civil and respectful. They have been, thanks in part to the presence of community access television."

When you have a minority group, topic, or idea that needs to be heard, recognized, and understood by the majority, try the Ask a *<u>fill-in-theblank</u>* panel discussion format.

19 THE LEGO® SERIOUS PLAY® FORMAT

It started with a bit of small talk. A party of local entrepreneurs were talking about how Serious Play methods and design thinking tools can support creativity and knowledge sharing and thereby accelerate innovation and value creation. Certified LEGO® Serious Play® facilitator, Dr. Camilla Nørgaard Jensen talked about how building a model can help unleash deep understanding and creativity. It should be no surprise that we also talked about panel discussions. And then we started brainstorming how we might integrate LEGO® Serious Play® into a panel discussion.

The LEGO® Serious Play® panel format is perfect for topics that are complex, have differing perspectives, or when opinions are difficult to access or deeply personal.

This model creates a visual anchor to represent ideas, thoughts, and feelings that may not otherwise be articulated in a group setting.

Here are a few nuances to this format that you'll need to consider.

DECIDE WHO WILL BE BUILDING THE MODEL

- *Just the panelists.* If you use this option, I suggest you have the panelists build their models right before start time OR have them working on building the models as the audience filters in, timing it so they are finished as you start the panel discussion.

- *Just the audience.* You'll want to have them seated at tables – rounds are best – with four to six people working on their individual model. If this is the case, you'll want to have the panelists working at a table or have the panelists each working at different tables. Once the models have been built, introduce the panelists. (You could also have each table send one representative of their group to be a panelist.)

- *Panelists and audience.* This is probably the easiest to do with a small group (less than 50).

BUY THE KITS

- You'll need to buy a LEGO® Serious Play® Starter Kit for each panelist or small group that will build a model. There are 214 pieces specifically created for their metaphorical value.

- Have them ready to go. (Jensen suggests you put the turntables, hinges and tires together ahead of time, put each kit in a separate plastic bag, and make the kits easily accessible.)

THINK THROUGH THE LOGISTICS OF DEBRIEFING THE MODEL

- For small groups, most audience members will be able to see the models—either up front on the stage or on the table tops.

- For larger groups, it may be difficult to see the models as they are debriefed. If this is the case, you may want to learn if your A/V crew can produce a live video feed of the models as they are being presented.

THINK ABOUT HOW TO GET YOUR LEGO® PIECES BACK

- People get attached to their models, so you may decide to gift the model to the panelists. Either way, bring plastic zipper bags or sealable containers to store the individual kits.

- For the audience members, encourage them to take a picture, tweet it (provide your Twitter handle if you would like to be tagged. Encourage hashtags such as #LEGOSeriousPlay), and then put all the pieces back in the bag/box. Yes, you literally have to tell them, remind them, and tell them again.

HOW TO FACILITATE LEGO® SERIOUS PLAY®

STEP 1   **INTRODUCE THE MODEL**
- Welcome and introduce how this will be a novel panel format. Explain what will happen.
- Outline the LEGO® Serious Play® method and the ground rules.

STEP 2   **DO A FEW WARM UPS**
- Take them through a couple of warm up exercises to help them understand how to build in metaphors. (Just Google "LEGO® Serious Play® skill building exercises" for ideas.)

STEP 3   **BUILD THE MODELS**
- Pose a question, a prompt, a topic or something that will spark conversation.
- Ask the panelists or audience (depending on the size) to use the LEGO® sets to build a metaphorical model that enables them to share their perspectives on the current question or topic. Reinforce that it is a metaphorical model—not a literal model. Encourage them to be creative and let their hands do the thinking. Offer an example, to clarify the process
- Give them three to six minutes to build the models, depending on the complexity of the question or topic. Instill a sense of urgency to induce a focused, non-analytic building session. You may choose to let them build in silence or provide background music.

STEP 4   **SHARE THE MODELS**
- If models are built at tables, ask for the group to select a spokesperson to share the model.
- In a roundtable fashion, ask each spokesperson to share the story of the model. Ask them to point to specific parts of the model—what did they build into the model and what does it represent? (A long LEGO® connector piece works well as a pointer.) Request that all listen generously; there is no question of correctness. There is no right or wrong model; no better or worse model. They are simply models to help the owner (panelist or small groups) describe what the topic means to them. There should be no interruptions while they are explaining.
- The panelists (or other participants) then get to ask clarifying questions about something they can physically observe in the model (not their interpretation). If time is an issue (when is it not?), give them a timeframe for the debriefing (2 minutes per table, otherwise, they may ramble or share EVERYTHING about their model).
- The panelists then have a discussion about common themes, differences of opinions, and any surprises and interesting discoveries.

STEP 5   **OPTIONAL - DEBRIEF THE EXPERIENCE**
- What just happened? What was it like for you? How was it different from a normal panel?
- Why does that matter? What are the impacts? How else might we...?

> You can do this if the panelists are physically co-located. Even better when you have small groups physically co-located. Make sure the LEGOs® ready to go. LEGO® sets can be sent to locations ahead of the virtual meeting.

20 SPOTLIGHT PANEL FORMAT

First featured by the ultimate panel destination, San Diego ComicCon, the Spotlight Panel session is exactly what it sounds like: a panel that spotlights one person.

So here's the funny part: A panel with one person is typically called an interview.

Although, you could spotlight two (or *maybe* three) partners, your c-suite team, or…use your imagination!

It's a very small panel that gets up close and personal.

Along with all the other virtual techniques, create visual variety with a virtual background that matches the segment of the panel. For example, when the panel moves to Q&A, the moderator and panelist(s) switch their virtual backgrounds.

Or have a "two camera" set up so the panelist can toggle between different camera views.

Or have the panelist take us on a "tour" of their room, office, or house.

CLASSIC DEBATE STYLE FORMAT 21

Everyone loves a good debate especially if there's a strong sense of an even-handed process. Facilitated by a skilled moderator, there are opportunities for the audience to get involved in the conversation, and they get to vote on who wins.

Let's take a page from the classic Oxford Union debate format and make it work in a panel discussion:

- Opening remarks. The panel moderator opens with a few words about the topic, process and voting procedures. The moderator introduces the panelists by name with a short one or two line introduction, which can be either humorous or serious. The moderator then calls on the first panelist to begin the debate.
- First panelist speaks for the proposition for a predetermined period of time. (I suggest no more than four minutes.)
- The moderator thanks the first panelist and calls upon the next panelist.
- The second panelist speaks for the opposition for the same predetermined time.
- The moderator thanks the panelist and then opens the debate from the floor. This is the opportunity for the audience to join in the debate. A certain amount of time will be allocated to this and each comment will be limited to an agreed maximum length of time.
- The moderator ends the floor debate and calls upon the next panelist.
- The third panelist speaks for the proposition for a predetermined period of time.
- The moderator thanks the third panelist and calls upon the next panelist.
- The fourth panelist speaks for the opposition for a predetermined period of time.
- The moderator thanks the panelist and calls for rebuttal remarks for a predetermined amount of time (typically half of the length of the first round of remarks). Rebuttals are usually made by the first and second panelists.
- The moderator calls an end to the debate and calls for the voting to begin.
- Audience votes by a show of hands or other polling procedure.

Sounds pretty simple, as long as you follow the structure without being too draconian! Oh, and the audience may only interrupt your debate using a Point of Information or a Point of Order:

POINT OF INFORMATION. An audience member wants to clarify or question a piece of information raised by a panelist, not to express an opinion. Here's the kicker: The panelist can choose to accept or refuse a point of information. Answering a few makes things a little livelier and more interactive, but taking too many interrupts the flow of your arguments.

POINT OF ORDER. An audience member wants to draw attention to an alleged violation or breach of the panel's rules of order (set by the moderator at the beginning). Like the point of information, a panelist must give way to a point of order.

Finally, remind your panelists that the goal of the debate is to inform and to win the votes of the audience. This involves more than making the best logical arguments. A few well-placed jokes, anecdotes and flat out pandering to the audience can often win votes and make it more interesting to attend.

22 HAT DEBATE FORMAT

When your panelists have differing viewpoints, try this hat debate format inspired by Jordan Weissmann at The Slate. He was frustrated with the healthcare discussion and proposed the following solution:

"From this day forward, whenever we discuss healthcare on TV, they should be broken up into three teams...If it were up to me, I would require them to wear hats with their team name, because it'd be vaguely funny, would probably help people remember the battle lines, and would even the playing field."

Weissmann defined the topic to fall into three main buckets:

- *The single-payer diehards* who want to pass Medicare for All.
- *The Obamacare lifers* who want to improve the Affordable Care Act.
- *The in-betweeners* who want to move more aggressively toward a true Medicare-style national health program that everybody can sign up for but don't want to annihilate the private insurance industry.

Regardless of your politics, you can use this example to inspire a little pizazz on your panel when you have a topic that lends itself to some sort of bucketing or categorization.

Tell your panelists you have selected three (or two or four) groups and that they will be arguing as a team, defending the broad contours of their approach. Ask them to pick their team, ostensibly preventing the panelists who've intentionally kept things vague on where they stand because we'll literally be able to see where they're standing. And their hats.

Weissmann agrees that there are "downsides to the company softball game approach to public policy debate. First off, the in-betweeners don't agree with each other on everything, which might lead to some internal squabbling that could bring down the whole team. Second, they'd probably need a better name[s] for their hats. But you get the idea."

Weissmann theorizes that "if you force all of them into a room, though, I'm sure they can come up with a compromise. I mean, if they can't negotiate that, there's no way they're ever going to hash out a healthcare bill with Capitol Hill."

Perhaps you can have an interesting debate discovering the nuances and differences in the topic using hats.

Be very specific about what hat they should wear (style, color, etc.). Otherwise, mail them what you want them to wear.

CROSSFIRE DEBATE FORMAT 23

There are plenty of political debate formats. My personal favorite is taken from the political commentary television show *Crossfire*. For the Crossfire format, determine:

- Whether you want a neutral panel moderator and diverse panelists or you want to stay true to the Crossfire format where each side of the aisle (liberal and conservative) serves as the moderator for each question.

- Then create a list of 20 provocative questions/statements related to the topic. Distribute them to the panelists as part of your pre-work or as they arrive.

Here's a crisp format to use:

- Welcome, Format Overview, Agenda and Ground Rules. Moderator clearly restates the topic to be discussed. (2 mins)

- Moderator (or Panelist A) introduces one of the statements and A explains agreement or disagreement and why. (1 min)

- Moderator (or Panelist A) solicits points of view from other panelists, particularly those with differing opinions. (4 mins)

- Moderator (or Panelist A) asks the audience (live and virtual) for feedback. (4 mins)

- Moderator (or Panelist A) refocuses or asks Panelist B to pick another question. (5 mins)

- Moderator (or Panelist B) introduces one of the statements and B explains agreement or disagreement and why. (1 min)

- Moderator (or Panelist B) solicits points of view from other panelists, particularly those with differing opinions. (4 mins)

- Moderator (or Panelist B) asks for audience feedback. (4 mins)

- Moderator (or Panelist B) refocuses or asks Panelist C to pick another question. (5 mins)

- Moderator (or Panelist C) introduces one of the statements and explains agreement or disagreement and why. (1 min)

- Keep the rotation going. You should be able to pose and discuss at least 6 provocative questions.

- At 2 minutes before ending, have the moderator or a panelist summarize the discussion. Say your thank yous and provide any administrative directions. (2 mins)

- Adjourn and have a great day—knowing that you have incited discussion in the hallways after such an exhilarating panel discussion.

> Because the virtual panel may not have the sides aligned next to each other, encourage each side to wear something (e.g. a specific color) that signifies their unity. Or send your panelists something to wear that's visible from the waist up – with each team wearing a different color shirt or hat. Makes a nice keepsake after the panel as well.

CASE STUDY
DEBATE STYLE FORMAT

The International Association of Professional Congress Organisers' (IAPCO) 2017 Annual Meeting in Dubai held a panel discussion in an unusual debate-style panel format.

The panel session was set up as a debate over the question of whether professional congress organizers (PCOs) should collaborate or compete in order to best serve clients, DMOs, and themselves.

Panelists were invited to represent either collaboration or competition; five of the six panelists chose collaboration and one spoke in favor of competition. The panelists were also asked to prepare their case, highlighting the benefits, evidence, and facts for their side during the debate.

Each panelist presented their viewpoint and then the moderator turned the tables, asking each panelist to argue against their original position. (Nope, they did *not* know the moderator was going to do this.)

"Suddenly, the audience and panelists were on the edge of their chairs," said panelist Jaimé Bennett of Conference Partners. "Those that had to switch sides not only had to think on their feet, but deliver their new argument with conviction."

The audience, seated at tables, also was asked to summarize their arguments for and against, flipping their original viewpoints.

Throughout the debate, the moderator would ask questions from the audience to loop them into the discussion

Discussion points were recorded by a graphic facilitator/artist on an engagement wall.

So who won?

"As we were moving along, we realized little by little that the borderline between the two positions was not so defined and fixed," said Bruna Bertolini, key account director, MCI France, who attended the session. "We concluded that in some situations we are ready to collaborate and in others we prefer to compete—it all depends on the context." But in the end, as evidenced by the list of benefits illustrated for each, collaboration won out over competition.

"It was a great session that highlighted that when reviewing a bid, we need to consider if collaborating is an option or if there is an opportunity to share knowledge with another company to assist with success," Bennett said. "To be able to collaborate, everyone agreed that trust, clear communication on roles and responsibilities, and 100% transparency are the key elements to ensure success." Bertolini agreed, "It is crucial also to determine clear tasks assignment and an exit policy."

This turn-the-tables debate format made the panel discussion more interesting and engaging for all.

CHAPTER THREE
FIND AND PREPARE D.E.E.P PANELISTS

*Just as you would plan the ultimate dinner party, you need the right mix of expertise,
ability to express an opinion coherently and divergent points of view.*

~ Ian Griffin

WHEN PUTTING TOGETHER a powerful panel, round up a handful of interesting people with different experiences and perspectives. In other words, look for **D.E.E.P** panelists:

DIVERSE. Beware of lining up a panel that is too similar and/or comfortable with each other. A group in complete agreement makes for a boring panel. A panel who knows each other well may lack a fresh perspective. And don't forget about visual diversity. A panel who looks too homogenous may not reflect the diversity within the audience.

EXPERTISE. Ask a recognized authority, influencer or thought leader within the industry who possesses strong enough credentials to generate credibility quickly through a bio or 30 second introduction. Or find a practitioner who has firsthand knowledge about the topic and has applied it successfully (or not) in the real world. You can also consider stakeholders—those representatives along the value chain. Invite a high-profile end-user customer, an employee or a vendor-partner who has expertise on the topic.

ELOQUENT. Panelists should be good conversationalists. How good are they on the phone? Was it a monologue or a discussion? Can they express their opinion and take a controversial position on a topic without being a jerk? Review video footage to make sure the potential panelist has the ability to keep the audience engaged and interested.

PREPARED. Some high profile personalities have one speech and won't (or cannot) tailor their presentation and/or comments for your specific audience or topic. Find someone who will do the work—who will have three key messages the audience needs to hear complemented with an anecdote, metaphor, analogy, example, or illustration specifically for them.

Warning: Just because someone recommends a panelist, doesn't mean they will be brilliant discussing your topic in front of your audience. Don't forget to do a little due diligence. Research their backgrounds through LinkedIn and Google. Get to know their points of view on the topic and as much as you can about their interests and background. Reach out to others in your network who know or are connected to them in some way and can tell you frankly amazing stories.

A FEW WORDS ABOUT VISUAL DIVERSITY

I see it all the time. A panel lacking visual diversity. It's a bunch of middle-aged white men with no women, minorities, or various ethnicities. In fact, there is a new term for all-male panels. It's a "manel" and they've gone viral via a Tumblr blog sarcastically called, *Congrats! You Have an All-Male Panel.*

Started in February 2015, the blog "documents all male panels, seminars, events, and various other things featuring all male experts." It features over 200 photos submitted from people from about ten countries. It's actually kind of funny because each photo has a witty call-out from David Hasselhoff. (Not an endorsement by David, just parody.)

Don't get me wrong. I like men. I'm even married to one. And a manel is absolutely fine if the panel discussion is at the Middle Aged White Guys Convention.

But most conferences and conventions have a diverse audience. I firmly believe the panel should represent the audience—not just with visual diversity, but with diversity of opinions, backgrounds and experiences. My experience is that meeting organizers:

- Simply don't think about it.

- Round up the people they know.

- Say they can't find anyone.

- Don't bother to look for anyone with the right credentials.

It's incumbent on meeting organizers to make sure there is visual *and* thought diversity on the platform—not just during panels, but throughout the event. As a panel moderator, many times I am handed a confirmed list of panelists. I may not have much influence over the selection, but I do point it out if there is a diversity issue. Perhaps there isn't diversity in this segment, but what about the rest of the program?

There are talented women and experts of various ethnicities who can be on panels or even moderate panels. (*Ahem,* that is a bold reference to my skill as a professional panel moderator.) You just have to go find them.

> Since the virtual panel is a much more visual medium, you simply can't discount the importance and power of virtual visual diversity.

AIM HIGH! 24

I was talking with a meeting organizer the other day who was grousing about the usual suspects. You know them. The folks who are ALWAYS called upon to be on a panel: legends in the business (at least in their own mind), panel groupies who always offer to be on a panel, sponsors needy to be recognized, and other folks who crave a tad bit of visibility (and you don't want to give them an entire breakout session).

You want your panelists to be **D.E.E.P.** (**D**iverse, have **E**xpertise, be **E**loquent and **P**repared), so don't settle for warm leftovers. Aim high!

After all, if you don't ask the people you really want to have on the panel, they can't possibly say "Yes".

Here are some ways to find great panelists:
- Put yourself in the audience's shoes. Who would they want to hear? Rather than assume, go ask a sample set of attendees.
- Ask your organizational heavy hitters who you should ask to be on the panel.
- Invite the keynote speaker to be part of a panel discussion about the conference theme.
- Google influencers and thought leaders. Invite them to participate directly or ask someone in your network who knows them to invite them.
- Look at your network and ask people you respect and admire to participate. Industry analysts, association leaders, and bloggers are good choices.
- Put out a call for panelists on your social networks.

And here are some ways you and the meeting organizer can sweeten the pot to inspire them to say "Yes":
- If they are authors, offer to hold a book signing.
- If they are speakers, offer to professionally videotape the session. It's always hard to get good, high quality video.
- If they are bloggers, influencers, or thought leaders, offer to make specific media mentions about the event and something they care about, such as their blog or upcoming public event.
- If PR is important to them, offer an extra press-only session
- If they are interested in making valuable connections, offer to host a *meet the panelists* reception or dinner or host an extra-special VIP private dinner.
- If they are looking for more visibility, offer to share (or help them create) a case study about how their customers have been successful using their products or services.
- Highlight the benefits of being a panelist, which is similar to the benefits of being a panel moderator:
  - *Stand Out.* Build a name for yourself in the industry and/or company.
  - *Meet Influencers.* Connect with fellow panelists.
  - *Get Smart.* It forces you to get up to speed on key trends that impact your industry and the particular issue being discussed.
  - *Reach New Customers.* Invite new and potential customers to attend the panel discussion. Let them know how it went and summarize the key points discussed.
  - *Credibility and Prestige.* Being on stage sends the message that you are someone with whom to do business.

- *Showcase Depth of Expertise.* Providing great information with great value allows you to demonstrate our expertise without having to be promotional.

- *Appreciation.* When you provide great value, the audience will appreciate you. They'll remember your name and buy from you and your company.

- *Awareness.* Being on a panel serves as a great icebreaker or conversation starter to meet people the rest of the conference.

Don't settle for ordinary. Delight the audience by aiming high, and bringing in new and fresh perspectives.

Expand your circle of potential panelists
by bringing in a remote panelist via livestream.

CAST FOUR PANELIST ROLES 25

In addition to selecting **D.E.E.P.** (**D**iverse, have **E**xpertise, be **E**loquent and **P**repared) panelists, where possible, you also want to cast for contrast. You are creating a scene, a panelesque, a movie. So you want different characters instead of everybody being the same.

According to Brian Walter, founder of Extreme Meetings, there are four basic roles you want to cast for:

1. **THE SAGE.** The sage is a combination of Dr. Phil, Judge Judy, and Yoda all mixed together.

2. **THE RELATER.** The relater is someone just like the majority of people in the audience, only more successful or at least slightly more successful. The audience is going to relate to them because they are thinking, "Oh my gosh, that panelist is just like me!"

3. **THE EXOTIC.** You want someone who is different, who will bring a unique perspective. The audience will be thinking, "I never thought of it like that before. That's interesting..."

4. **THE WILD MAN/WOMAN.** You want panelists that people have no idea what they're going to say next. It could be exciting. It could be insightful. It could be irreverent. It could be naughty. Thought-provoking. Funny! You don't actually know, so every time they speak, you'll be surprised and thinking, "What's going to happen?"

When you cast for these four roles, while making sure you have D.E.E.P. panelists, you're sure to have a winning panel discussion.

26 LIMIT THE NUMBER OF PANELISTS

I simply don't understand the thinking of putting a dozen panelists in a panel discussion format that will last an hour.

Just do the math: 5 minutes for the intro and 5 for the summary. That leaves 50 minutes divided by 12. This gives each panelist about four minutes of airtime—as long as the moderator doesn't say anything and the audience doesn't ask any questions. Bottom line: 12 is too many.

But what's the optimal number?

One person makes for an interview not a panel. A completely legitimate format, but it's not a panel.

Two people create an intimate conversation, especially if they have differing (even opposing) viewpoints. It can appear to be a debate (pro/con, he said/she said, point/counterpoint) or just a fireside chat.

Personally, I like *three* people with differing viewpoints; three just seems to be a magical number. It brings a conversational tone to the stage.

However, one person might drop out unexpectedly at the last minute for whatever reason. So inviting *four* panelists to participate is a smart move—just in case.

Five is bordering on the too many realm. Let's do the math again, but let's make sure the audience has some time to ask questions: five minutes for the introduction, a minimum of 15 minutes for Q&A and five minutes to summarize—which leaves a paltry 35 minutes for panelist discussion. That's no more than seven minutes per panelist on a good day. Borderline too many. Doable if you need a broad range of representation, but it's not optimum.

Six panelists? It just doesn't make sense from the panelist point of view (is this really worth my time going to this? Preparing for it? Especially when I won't have much airtime?) and the audience's point of view. (Why are they here if they don't say anything?) From the moderator's point of view, it's more challenging to firmly and respectfully intervene as the group gets larger.

Do everyone a favor, pick three or four articulate panelists with diverse viewpoints so there can be meaningful conversation among the panelists and with the audience.

KNOW THY PANELISTS 27

I just hate it when a moderator appears clueless about the topic or the panelists' contributions or points of view.

It's seems like they just showed up and expected to pull off a grand show! Ain't gonna happen.

Once you have identified the panelists:

DO YOUR HOMEWORK. Google their work and views they hold on the topic. Review the panelists' websites, social profiles, books, reviews, bios, blogs, recent presentations, media mentions, papers, and other sources that will help you understand their perspectives.

TAKE NOTES. You don't need to know *everything* about the panelists' lives, but you should have a basic idea of their position on the topic. This will make it much easier to connect with and introduce each panelist.

TALK TO EACH PANELIST. Schedule some time to talk either by phone or F2F and discuss:

- *Expectations.* Let them know what to expect (go over the format) then ask them about their experiences with panels.

- *Audience.* Share the demographics and experience level of the intended audience.

- *Content.* Given the topic, ask them what they would like to talk about. Tease out the juicy bits from the audience's point of view. Look for possible areas of contention with the other panelists' points of view.

- *Rapport.* As you talk to each of the panelists, you are not only assessing their speaking strengths, style and perspectives; you are also creating a connection and building trust.

28 PREPARE YOUR PANELISTS

A recipe for panel disaster is allowing panelists (not just the moderator) to just show up and expect brilliance to spring forth. Sure, it could happen if the panelists are socially aware, have met each other before, and are willing to stay focused on the topic. But without preparation, it probably won't go so well.

I'm a big fan of preparing panelists ahead of time about the process we'll be using—and less about the content. If you talk too much about the topic beforehand, you've already had the panel discussion and the audience loses out on the spark and spontaneity of live interaction. It's a delicate balance.

And I never, ever, assume panelists have served on a panel discussion before.

Here are my suggestions on how to prepare your panelists to be absolutely brilliant on game day:

PRE-EVENT EMAIL. Confirm these details to make sure they are clear about expectations and comfortable with their role:

- *The Promise.* Confirm the title, date, time, location, description, objectives and promotional material.

- *The Panelists.* Share the names, short bios and websites of all the panelists, where to register and where to meet up just prior to their session.

- *The Format.* Describe how you plan to run the panel and the first one or two questions you intend to ask.

- *The Audience.* Share audience demographics and estimated size so panelists can bring the appropriate number of handouts, books, or other things they'd like members of the audience to have.

- *The Room.* Describe the backdrop, chairs, platform configuration, and if water will be available.

- *Presentations.* Provide specific instructions, for example, time frames, slide format, getting the slides to you, any other instructions.

- *Audio/Visual.* Explain the venue's A/V capabilities and determine any additional requirements such as microphones, coordination of video, or whether it will be recorded.

- *Promotion.* Declare the degree of appropriate self-promotion as well as use of social media.

- *Pre-Event Call.* Have a short conference or video call to allow everyone to connect and hear this same information.

- *Quick Meet Up.* Meet about an hour before the event to go over the format and any last minute issues.

PRE-EVENT MEET UP. A short conference call or video conference (30 minutes) a week before the panel allows the opportunity for everyone to connect and hear the same information sent in the email as well as ask any format questions. *You don't want to conduct the panel beforehand, so keep this light and social.* If you believe there might be a lack of controversy or potential overlap in answers or opinions, you *may* want to probe each panelist's approach to the topic. It's also a nice touch to invite the meeting organizer to attend or to listen in. Here are some key items to cover:

- *Welcome.* Set the tone for how excited you are.

- *Panel Information.* Panel title and objectives.

- *Self-Introductions.* Name and two sentences about their expertise, approach, or opinion. Be firm in enforcing the two sentence rule—you are modeling being an effective facilitator.

- *Audience.* Review the audience demographics and size.

- *Panel Format.* Review the format/agenda.

- *Questions.* Share the first few questions you will ask during the panel and see if there are any questions they want you to ask.

- *Props.* Encourage props or items to help the conversation or illustrate a key point.

- *Other?* Open the floor for any questions from the panelists.

- *Event Meet Up.* Confirm the time and location (speaker lounge, green room, or other space that has some privacy) to meet about an hour before the event to go over last minute issues.

FINAL CONFIRMATION. Take notes during the pre-event meet up and email them to all panelists. This also serves as an excellent final confirmation of their participation.

BREAK BREAD. Invite the panel to go to breakfast, lunch or dinner together, especially if they have not met. This is meant to be an opportunity to relax, get to know each other and build a rapport that will be obvious on stage. It is not the place to hold the panel discussion.

TOUCH BASE. As soon as you get to the venue, seek out your panelists to say hello. Help them get settled, remind them of the objective and ground rules, and answer any last minute questions they may have. Chances are they don't need your help, but they will appreciate the effort—and it allows them to be brilliant on stage.

MEET UP RIGHT BEFORE. 45–60 minutes before the panel discussion is to start, the panel moderator and the panelists should meet each other F2F for about 15 minutes. If a panelist cannot attend, you should make other arrangements to get together onsite prior to the session. The point of this meet-up is to make sure they are all present and accounted for, answer any final questions, ensure they are relaxed and prepared to have some fun! At this quick meeting the panel moderator should:

- Review the format and agenda. Be firm with panelists about the amount of time allocated to their initial comments and other ground rules.

- It's a nice touch to hand out the agenda on one side and on the other side have the seating plan and top five ground rules.

- Review the seating order and make sure it is consistent with your prepared slide.

- Review your introduction with each panelist for accuracy and relevance. Make sure you know how to pronounce their personal and company names correctly.

- Encourage panelists to treat this like a conversation.

- Tell them how and when you will intervene and how they should signal to you or each other when they want to answer a question or add to the discussion.

- Remind panelists to turn off their cell phones.

- Encourage panelists to mingle with the crowd before the session starts and to have fun!

Resist the urge to discuss what you are going to talk about.

You want to keep the conversation fresh and lively so the panel discussion doesn't feel like warmed up leftovers!

Follow the same guidelines as above, including specific instructions about staging and technology.

29 HELP PANELISTS BE MEMORABLE

So you're talking to your panelists in preparation for an amazing panel discussion, and one of your panelists ask, "What can I do to make an impact? To be memorable so that people DO something with the information?"

*Ah...*and that's the challenge, isn't it?

We can have lovely conversations, but at the end of the day, what's the point?

Here's the deal: We all want to witness a unique conversation you can't get anywhere else, so it's important to continuously reinforce a conversational tone to the panel so it doesn't sound stiff or rehearsed.

To do that, the panelists need to come prepared:

- Be ready to share two or three key messages for the audience to derive great value.
- With each of these key messages, identify an example, a story, demonstration, or prop that makes that idea come to life.
- Come up with a short, Twitterable sound bite audiences will remember later.
- Prepare a final takeaway, insight, or idea you want to leave the audience with. I'm a big fan of asking the audience to do something—a call to action—based on what they heard.

When the panelists come prepared, they will be able to be more conversational and provide greater value to the audience.

CREATE A VISUAL KEEPSAKE 30

Erin L. Albert suggested this tip to have a Unicorian, Utterly Unforgettable Panel Discussion. She noted, "The organizer of the panel gave the panelists something interesting to wear to mark the occasion. This may seem trite or silly, but trust me, it's not. It's probably one of the BEST items for panelists and the audience to have a mental avatar of your panel discussion. They'll remember it."

What's a visual keepsake? Here are some examples: For a panel on gender parity, the panelists wore an embroidered purple sash that said #Manbassador. Another panel of women bloggers wore bright orange boas.

Having a wearable avatar does four things for you and your panelists:

1. It identifies the panelists in a crowd for discussion after the event.
2. It provides panelists with a visible symbol of the talk which they can take home and put in their offices, and provide a mental hallmark of the day.
3. It's GREAT for social media and photos.
4. Word of mouth endures long after the event.

So help your panelists be memorable and feel special with a visual keepsake.

> Send your panelists something to wear that's visible from the waist up.
> Or ask them to wear a specific color especially when
> you have your panelists debating specific positions.

31 HELP BUSY EXECUTIVES PREPARE

Let's get real. What are the odds of getting executives together to prepare for your upcoming panel discussion? Shockingly low.

As the panel moderator, you absolutely know the key to success is in the preparation. Here's the challenge: Most moderators email the executives saying something like, "I want to go over some of the question formats and things that we'll be doing with the panel *blah blah blah blah*." Gee, here's a surprise. They never call you back. They're going to be dismissive because it's not about you, even though you're trying to help them. Why? You don't share what's in it for them.

I know. You really want to say, "Excuse me, I'm your panel moderator. We need to get together, so you don't look foolish." No, you can't be that brazen, but you *can* approach them individually. Call the gatekeeper and/or send an email that says, "I'm going to ask a few prepared questions in such a way that you can come across looking brilliant. Do you have five minutes to chat?" Oh yes, now they'll talk to you.

Brian Walter, founder of Extreme Meetings suggests, "Every executive has a pet project. Every leader has a pet initiative. Find out what it is because they want to advance that initiative. When you can tie what they want to what you want to cover then it's going to work. Let's say they're talking about how to speed up our rate of closing. So, I want to ask them questions about how quickly we can change the culture of closing in your organization. 'Do you have five minutes to talk about that?' They will always, always, always say "Yes". Then you can prep them with question formats because they see the value of it. You must always make it about them."

Most executives are extremely busy and intend to look over their notes on the plane trip to the conference. Make sure you prep them well so they can provide tremendous value to the audience and look brilliant during the panel discussion.

MANAGE THE SLIDES 32

One of my panelists *insisted* that she needed to show slides. Considering that slides are usually for presentations and the one unforgivable offense of a panel is to rise and give a speech, I did *not* entertain her request. Panels should focus on the discussion and interaction between panelists and not on a humongous screen.

That being said, there can be some instances when slides can be appropriate and add a bit of pizazz to the panel:

- *Adds value* from the attendee's perspective.
- Makes an abstract concept *more visibly understandable*.
- Grabs the audience's *attention*.

Here are some specific examples where I think it can be appropriate to have a slide or few:

- *Panelist Slide.* One slide for each panelist with a photograph, name, a few key bullets and Twitter handle. Display this slide when the panelist is introduced. Create a continuous loop of all the panelist slides to show as people are walking into the room, prior to the start of the session.
- *Panelist Summary Slide.* One slide with each panelist lined up in the same seating order with photo, headline and Twitter handle. This may stay up for the duration of the session.
- *Transition.* A funny, applicable video transition as the panel is getting set up or right after it is over.
- *Reference.* Allow all panelists to submit one slide they may need to reference during the conversation. If you allow more, then allow all the panelists the same number of slides.

If you *are* going to allow panelists to present using visuals:

- Set a maximum number of slides and amount of time. A 60-minute panel can use 15–20 slides and a panelist should speak to only two or three slides before giving the floor to another panelist.
- Keep the slides brief and specific to the topic. Consider having additional information in a handout, takeaway, or on a website rather than in the slides.
- Use the organization's defined format or template, if required.
- Include the panelist's contact name and information on the first slide.
- Keep the slideshow from being dependent on Wi-Fi. Although it may be accessible, it may not work.
- Use video judiciously. It can gobble up precious time quickly.

As a moderator, assemble *one* overall slideshow file and be responsible for advancing the slide deck. You'll want to make sure the slides address the topic, comply with your slide count max, and minimize duplication among the panelists' presentations. Preload the file on a single computer to eliminate the technical difficulties in making multiple laptops work with a single projector. Then, as the panelists speak, you (or the A/V tech) can easily bring up and advance the slides.

Finally, beware of the clever panelist who wants to show a slide or video at the very last minute. Your answer should be a firm and pleasant "No". You didn't really want slides for your panel discussion anyway.

Prepare ONE slide deck that either you or the technician controls. Fussing with devices will trump your ability to keep the conversation flowing.

33 HAVE A HANDOUT OR TAKEAWAY

The ultimate purpose of a handout or takeaway should be to enhance the panel, not detract from the discussion. So what's the difference? This should help:

> **A HANDOUT** is printed material that supports the discussion. It can be in the form of an agenda, an outline, PowerPoint slide printouts, fact sheets, a list of references, a spreadsheet, or an article handed out prior to or during the session. It can also include promotional materials about you, your panelists, their organizations, or a specific product or service that would benefit the audience.
>
> **A TAKEAWAY** can be the same thing as your handout, just a summary, or some other gift; the only difference is that it's given to attendees as they leave the meeting.

One reason handouts exist is so that the audience can take notes during the panel discussion. When people write things down, they are also more likely to remember the salient points, even if they never go back and look at their notes again. Handouts also provide audience members with a sense of security, especially during highly technical panel discussions, because they know that detailed information is there to refer to if necessary. As an added benefit to you, should your technology fail, you can always rely on your handouts.

Sounds like you should always have a handout, right? Not so fast; there are two sides to every coin. If you give the audience material to refer to while the panel talks, you run the risk of losing the attention of a large percentage of your audience. They will be looking at and reading the handout rather than listening to the panel. They will also be flipping ahead, trying to figure out what the panel *is going* to say rather than listening to what they *are* saying.

HAVE A HANDOUT STRATEGY

While there is no right or wrong answer, you do have choices when it comes to using handouts:

- Put the handouts on each chair or on the table at each place right before people come in.
- Distribute your handout as people walk in. The ushers at church do this quite efficiently.
- Distribute your handout at a specific moment during your presentation.
- Save your handout for the end of your speech. Now it's called a takeaway.
- Consider distributing your handout and any other supplemental information in PDF format on a flash drive or providing a Web page URL you encourage the audience to visit.

Figure out your strategy and tell the participants up front so they can know what to expect and it takes the burden off note taking if they know they are getting a handout. Unless, of course, you want it to be a surprise!

Send your handout either prior to or at the beginning of the panel discussion. Email the takeaway at the end or shortly thereafter.

CASE STUDY
ALIGNED PANELISTS

Kate Delaney moderated Creating and Curating Relevant and Valuable Content with panelists Patti Dennis, Vice President of TEGNA; Amy Cosper, Editor-in-Chief of Entrepreneur Magazine; Rachel Weintraub, Emmy nominated and award winning TV producer; and Heath Row, Research Operations Manager for Google at the National Speakers Association Annual Convention.

After the convention, Bill Cates, CSP, CPAE, wrote to me in an email: "While I don't usually like panels on the main stage with larger groups, this one was great. The right people, saying relevant things, lead in the right way. Extraordinary!"

Well, I had to find out what made it so extraordinary.

I asked Delaney, "Why do you think this went so darn well?"

Delaney responded, "I think the panelists were perfectly aligned because you had somebody from the print world, you had people who were recruiting, bringing in the digital and broadcast world, and you had a brilliant panelist in Heath Row from Google where they are curating and gathering all those statistics and trying to disseminate them and figure out what kind of content people are really craving and that combination of all of those panelists. I think pulling them together was really the brilliance of it and my role was to just be the extractor (not put myself in it) but just to extract those valuable pieces of information."

You can find out more about how Kate Delaney prepared to moderate this extraordinary panel in the case study at the end of Chapter 4.

CHAPTER FOUR
CURATE FABULOUS QUESTIONS

My philosophy about asking curated questions to the panel is that I will ask questions the audience would ask. I need to know enough about everyone on the panel and the topic so that I'm thinking in the same manner as the audience. They know that I've done my homework.

~ Scott McKain

THE KEY TO ANY GREAT PANEL discussion is for the moderator and audience to ask great questions that inspire frank conversation. In my experience, that doesn't happen spontaneously. Great questions are often curated in advance by the moderator or crowdsourced from the audience either before or during the panel discussion.

This chapter provides a process to gather interesting potential questions, select the best questions to ask, and to think about those questions where you want to probe a bit deeper. A well-prepared panel moderator has the flexibility to bend, adjust, and adapt to the ensuing conversation.

HOW TO CURATE QUESTIONS

STEP 1   ## DO YOUR RESEARCH
First, you'll want to do a bit of research on the topic, the panelists, other experts in the field, as well as the audience. As you research the topic, talk to the panelists and connect with the audience (either through social media or a few sample interviews), you'll start to compile a list of potential questions. These questions should be specifically:

- Tied to the topic.
- Reflective of a specific panelist's work or interests.
- Representative of issues the audience will be interested in.

At this point, don't worry about the exact phrasing of the questions. Prepare more questions than you think you'll need and make sure they cover the topical landscape.

STEP 2   ## LOOK AT YOUR LIST
When you're ready, pull out that long list of potential questions from your research.

- What's the most prevalent question on everyone's mind?
- Why is this topic important right now?
- What are the key challenges the audience is facing about this topic?
- What are the two things that are most important to share/discover on this topic during the panel?
- Where does the panel agree and disagree about the topic?

STEP 3   ## CULL YOUR LIST
Keep questions that will:

- Deliver the biggest and broadest impact and value from the audience's perspective.
- Address an issue, challenge, or capture the interest of the audience.
- Start a deeper conversation or spark an interesting debate.
- Uncover something the audience can't easily find on the internet.
- Provide valuable takeaway nuggets.

Whittle your list down to at least two main questions per panelist. Make sure they draw upon the panelist's expertise and experiences in a useful way. Keep a backup of ten or more questions to use if needed.

STEP 4   ## SANITY-CHECK YOUR QUESTIONS
When finalizing your questions, put yourself in your audience's shoes. Use your valued resources from step 1 and ask them to take a look at your draft list of questions:

- Is there something you would be interested in that I'm not asking or thinking about?
- Do you think these questions are relevant/good?
- What else should I add/consider?
- Which of these questions do you think I should dump?

STEP 5   **SEQUENCE THE QUESTIONS**

Typically, moderator-curated questions have a flow that moves from strategic to the more tactical:

- *Strategic.* Start with broad high altitude questions designed to discuss what is happening in the world.

- *Benefits.* Move to the benefits and/or consequences about why the audience should care.

- *Specifics.* Ask more specific questions where the panelists will be more inclined to share anecdotes or concrete examples.

- *Application.* Make sure the audience walks away with substantial value and the ability to apply the information.

STEP 6   **START STRONG**

The first question sets the tone for the panel, so you want to be thoughtful about how you start your questions:

- *Softie.* Warm up the panelists with broad, easy questions so the panelists can settle in and relax. Ask for a definition, talk about the history of the topic or why this topic is so interesting. Then raise the stakes, probing into more controversial areas.

- *Hardball.* Start out with a strong, provocative question. For example, ask each panelist, in 30 seconds or less, to offer a strong opinion on the topic.

- *Gauge the Room.* When the audience's skill level is not known, do some level-setting of the audience's experience. For example, ask for a show of hands, "How many people have less than two years of experience writing Java? Between two and five years? And those who think they should be on the panel rather than out in the audience?"

The first person to speak will also influence the tone of the panel, so consider carefully who you want to start with. Consider having the seating plan reflect your initial order.

STEP 7   **FINE-TUNE THE QUESTIONS**

Rephrase the questions (the shorter, the better) in order to position questions for panelists and audience and to keep everything on track.

STEP 8   **CREATE CUE CARDS**

You can write your questions down on 3"x5" or 5"x7" index cards (consider using a key-ring punched through the upper left-hand corner to keep the cards in order during the session) or use a tablet to scroll through your questions. You can also use them as prompts for your welcoming remarks, panelist introductions, and closing remarks.

Why go through all the hassle of curating some fabulous questions for your panelists?

Consider it as an insurance policy.

You may not even need to use many of them because the conversation flows easily. Other times, you may have to use every single one of them during a rather fitful panel discussion. You just don't know until you get there. So come prepared with fabulous moderator-curated questions.

34 COMMON QUESTION TYPES

Here are the 15 most common types of questions used during a panel discussion. There ARE more, but this is a good start. Perhaps you can use these formats to help curate your questions for your next panel discussion.

1. *Statement Plus a Question* that starts with a statement (or two) providing context for the question.

2. *Statement Contains a Quote* from the panelist, another panelist, expert or observer—and then followed up with a question.

3. *Statement Contains a Statistic* (an intriguing one) combined with a relevant question.

4. *Explain Your Position* with a brief summary of the panelist's position and the question as a request for further details for the benefit of the audience—usually to compare and contrast a specific position from the other panelists.

5. *Changed Your Mind* probes into the notion that a panelist's position (or world view) has changed over time. The moderator states the prior position with a follow-up question.

6. *Comment Question* where a panelist is asked to comment on a fellow panelist's position.

7. *Agree/Disagree?* A slight variation to commenting on a fellow panelist's position is a simple question: "Do you agree with a fellow panelist's position?" Of course, the other panelist will follow up with some commentary.

8. *Direct Question.* Sometimes, a question needs no embellishment. No statements, no quotes, no statistics—just the question.

9. *Repeat the Question.* When a question is so darn good, direct it to another panelist. *Note: use this hot-potato technique sparingly.*

10. *Hypothetical Question* is the proverbial What If question. What if…you had started sooner or later? Not doubted yourself? Had no customers? Kept your job? Could only use one hand? Tried to do this in 1995? Heard about a better option?

11. *Human Interest* question is slightly off-topic yet enables the audience to understand the panelist as an everyday human being.

12. *Give an Example* to provide a real-world story that provides more insight into the topic.

13. *Test the Unsaid* to test the waters to bring out an unspoken issue. "We seem to be skirting around the issue. Could it be Z?"

14. *Poll the Panelists* with a quick show of hands where a closed question is posed to the panel and all must indicate their position by raising their hand, waving a flag, or some other visual indicator showing their position.

15. *Lightning Round* where the moderator asks a question and then goes down the line of panelists asking for a one word/short answer from each panelist.

PROBE DEEPER WITH QUESTIONS 35

I was chatting with Dutch Driver, a colleague from my early days of facilitation (we actually used a listserv to communicate), about the power of asking a thought-provoking question during a panel discussion. It's really the Socratic Method at its best. Evidently, he has been curating a list of questions and is willing to share them with you. You may find some you can use during your next panel discussion (or conversation):

QUESTIONS FOR CLARIFICATION

- What do you mean by XXX?
- What is your main point?
- How does XXX relate to AAA?
- How can you phrase that differently?
- What do you think is the main issue here?
- Is your basic point XXX or AAA?
- What is an example of this?
- Would this be an example: XXX?
- How might you explain this further?
- What makes you say that?
- Let me see if I understand; do you mean XXX or AAA?
- How might this relate to our discussion problem/issue/question?
- What do you think Jamaal meant by his remark? Or What did you take Jamaal to mean?
- Joey, would you summarize in your own words what Jamaal has said? Jamaal, is that what you meant?

QUESTIONS THAT PROBE PURPOSE

- What is the purpose of XXX?
- What was your purpose when you said XXX?
- How do the purposes of these two people vary?
- How does the purpose of these groups vary?
- What is the purpose of the main character in this story?
- Was this purpose justifiable?
- Was the purpose addressing the question at this time?

QUESTIONS THAT PROBE ASSUMPTIONS

- What are you assuming here?
- What is John assuming?
- What assumptions could we use instead?
- You seem to be assuming XXX. Do I understand you correctly?
- All of your reasoning depends on the idea that XXX. Why have you based your reasoning on XXX rather than AAA?
- You seem to be assuming XXX. How do you justify taking this for granted?
- Is this always the case? What are the exceptions? How do you justify that these assumptions hold here?

Keep these questions in your back pocket, just in case you need them at your next panel discussion.

36 SHARE QUESTIONS IN ADVANCE

After a recent panel moderation, an audience member approached me and asked, "Did the panelists know the questions in advance?"

In this case, my answer was, "Yes, the panelists knew about 80% of the questions in advance. Why do you ask?"

"Just curious," was the response.

"*Ummmm…*did it *look* like the panelists were scripted?"

"No," he said. "Just curious."

Well, that got me thinking about precisely when I consider sharing all (or most) of the curated questions with the panelists. Here are the times I share most (not all) questions with panelists:

RISK. With some topics, there is a risk to having a more spontaneous reaction to a question. Especially when your panelist is a lawyer, executive, or celebrity. Anything they say reflects on them as an individual or as a representative of their organization. Saying something not intended (or permissible) makes it a risk.

EXPOSURE. If the session is being recorded or live-streamed, the risk factor increases exponentially. Keep in mind, everyone with a smartphone is a potential broadcaster, so the risk is always there.

PERSONAL CHOICE. Perhaps it's the first time a panelist is on a panel or the moderator is not as familiar with the industry or specific wording of the questions. By sharing the questions, it will make panelists and moderator more comfortable and confident.

For that particular panel, we hit the trifecta! As a result, I shared most of the prepared questions in preparation for an amazing panel discussion.

CASE STUDY
CURATED QUESTIONS

To continue our case study with Kate Delaney (see Chapter 3), I asked, "How did you get your panelists aligned?" Here's what she did:

RESEARCH. Delaney looked at the panelists' backgrounds through LinkedIn and Google. She reached out to others in her network who "knew or were connected to them in some way and could tell me really frankly amazing stories."

LOTS OF FEEDBACK. To get a list of starting questions, she reached out to conference organizers, five or so of her journalist friends who were intimately familiar with the topic, and five of her speaker buddies who essentially represented the audience. Delaney explains, "I put them together in my crew and I sent them out an email and said, 'Okay, you're in my circle. Will you all look at these questions? Is there something you would be interested in that I'm not asking or thinking about? Do you think these questions are relevant and good? What else can I squeeze in here or should I dump some of these questions?'"

A HANDFUL OF QUESTIONS. She then culled that list down to a handful or so. "I got rid of the questions I thought were just too narrow. I needed broader questions," keeping those that had the biggest and broadest impact and value from the audience's perspective.

PERSISTENCE. Especially with busy, important people, it's easy to have them blow off the preparation call. In this case, NSA's Director of Meetings and Events was dog-gone persistent. They finally picked a date, and then one of the panelists couldn't make it. So Delaney spent 1.5 hours on the phone with him the night before AND sent him a recording of the call! Talk about being persistent!

PREP WORK PAYS OFF. All the panelists, the moderator, and conference organizers got on a video conference call. "We had a conversation between all of us. Here's how the panel is going to go. Here's the general direction." Essentially, she modeled the conversational tone she was looking for on the panel without actually getting into the content of the discussion.

CONVERSATIONAL DRUMBEAT. Delaney continually emphasized the importance of making it like a conversation. How? "I pumped them up by saying 'We just want to have a conversation here. You are the barracudas. You have this incredible information. It's amazing we have you here! I just want to get as much out to this audience as we can in a conversational way.' [The conference organizers were] backing me up on that too during the call. [And right beforehand, I was saying] 'This is a conversation. Don't worry. Just let it flow. I'm not gonna get in the way. Just follow your instincts. Just have that conversation like we're all sitting around discussing something really valuable and important to the people who are listening. Don't be afraid to jump in. You have a point to make, or somebody says something and you don't agree, or you want to add to it, just go for it!' And they got that they completely understood it's conversational."

PRACTICE. Delaney moderated the whole panel without notes, cue cards, or teleprompter. She practiced in her office so she was completely comfortable with the format, the introductions, and sequence of questions, so that she could be completely present to the conversation in the moment.

A big shout out to Kate Delaney for sharing her wisdom and perspective on creating an amazing panel discussion at Influence '16.

CHAPTER FIVE
STAGING AND A/V TIPS

The setup of the room is important. Do you want to be in the middle of the panel looking to either side like Tony Jones on Q and A? Do you want to be seated centrally in the middle of the audience, like Drew Carey on Whose Line is it Anyway or the moderators of the US Presidential debates? Or do you want to stand at a podium next to the panel? All of these will shape the way you can command the attention of panelists and audience. The setup gives you another secret weapon. It is hard to confront somebody who is beside you. Compare sitting at a dinner table to standing at the front of a classroom. You can engineer this so that the most combative panelists are defused by sitting next to each other, or – if you want fireworks, sit them opposite each other and they'll easily get into battle.

~ Claire Duffy

THE DEFAULT PANEL ROOM SET appears to be a long table at the front of the room, draped with a white (or black) tablecloth with skirting. Corded microphones on a stand are at each panelist position or between panelists to share. The lectern is downstage right (or left). The audience is seated theater-style in rows.

Sigh.

Yet another typical panel discussion, probably chock-full of presentations, leaving just a few minutes for Q&A at the end.

Ho-hum.

Who wants to walk into a room like that? No life; no energy. Where's the *joie de vivre?* Don't default to stiff traditionalists. You can easily add a little pizazz by following a few of the staging and audio/visual (A/V) tips in this chapter.

37 MAKE THE ROOM ENGAGING

Make the room more engaging as the audience walks through the door. Here's a checklist of things to consider as you prepare the room:

TABLES. Have round tables that encourage discussion between attendees.

CHAIRS. If you have to do theater-style seating, consider audience-centered arrangements. Set the first row of chairs so they're close to the panelists. Face each chair directly toward the center of the panel and make sure each chair has an unobstructed view.

BARRIERS. Get rid of the traditional skirted table that separates the panel from the audience. Consider seating the panelists in comfortable chairs in a shallow semi-circle with small cocktail tables set to the sides.

STAGE. A raised stage can also separate the panel from the audience; however, it may be necessary to enable the back rows to see the panelists.

LIGHTING. Keep the house lights up, at least a half to two-thirds.

POSTERS. Post topic-related intriguing pictures, icons, phrases, quotations, charts etc. on the walls around the room. Post a welcome sign by the door.

MUSIC. Have some upbeat, popular, age-appropriate music playing as they enter. Don't forget to license the use of that music through ASCAP or BMI.

SLIDESHOW. Have a continuous looping file with bios and interesting tidbits of information about the topic including a hashtag for the event.

QUESTION CARDS. Pass out preprinted question forms or note cards to the audience as they walk in or have them placed on each chair as they enter the room.

MICROPHONES. For audiences less than 50 people, don't bother. Between 50–75, it's nice to have. Over 75, amplify the moderator, panelists and audience members who ask questions.

GREENERY. Put some live plants, decorations or a backdrop to make the stage more inviting. Project images of the company logo or meeting theme against the backdrop or to the sides of the stage. Be sure you don't project the images over the faces of the panelists.

CLUTTER. Right before the panel starts, take a last look around and remove any clutter. Old plastic water bottles, random tables, loose pieces of paper.

It's amazing how just a few little things can signify to the audience that they are going to be in good hands—that this is going to be special. You might even raise their expectations of the session.

Make the virtual room more engaging by having background music and/or a continuous looping slideshow playing as people enter the room. Moderators and panelists should have cameras on with a clean, interesting background clear of clutter.

DRESS UP THE ROOM AT NO COST 38

No one wants a boring draped table at the front of the room, but how do you dress up a setting without breaking the bank? It's a great question since many panel discussions have virtually no budget. So I called Deborah Molique, a consultant for in-house event teams at Molique.com in Scottsdale, AZ. Here's what we came up with:

FURNITURE AND FIXTURES

- *Borrow.* During your site visit, be on the lookout for furniture you can borrow: lounge furniture (matching chairs, couches, cocktail tables, or floor/table lamps) from the lobby, executive chairs from the sales office or board room, furniture in a room or suite, chairs from the hallway, highboys from the bar. While you're at it, look for potted plants, artificial trees, artwork, or anything else that sparks your fancy. Before you sign the contract with the meeting venue, negotiate use of the furniture to be used at no cost during the panel—and that the venue will move it to and from the room for you.

- *Bring it.* When the venue is dull and doesn't have anything to borrow, bring it from home or from a (nice) friend's house.

- *Buy it.* If you have a bit of a budget for speaker gifts, a nice touch is to buy and personalize director's chairs and then give them to the panelists as their gift for sharing their wisdom. Or shop at a low price furniture store and donate the items at the end of the event.

- *Sponsor.* Perhaps there's a local event furniture design store that might be interested in showcasing their wares in front of your audience? You never know until you ask.

- *Delete it.* I'm not a big fan of the draped table or even a cocktail table in front of the panelists. It creates a physical barrier between them and the audience. So you gotta ask yourself, "Do we even need that table?" You might want to put some small tables between the panelists or behind them to place a pitcher of water.

BACKDROP

- *Media Wall.* Does your organization have a step and repeat media wall they use for photo, branding, or award opportunities? If so, borrow it from the entrance just in time for your panel. If not, they're fairly reasonable to purchase and can be used and reused in a variety of ways. Have them printed on both sides (one with a dark background and the other side with a light background) to create more visual interest. (Think selfies!)

- *Welcome Signage.* Many organizations have some kind of welcome signage or retractable banner signs at the entrance of the event. Move those to your room just in time for your panel.

- *Multimedia Screen.* If the room comes with multimedia capability, design an interesting slide with the topic, speaker photos, and information. Spend some time to make it look classy (vs. boring) and you won't have to take as much time on introducing the panelists.

- *Wallpaper.* You can also design some inspirational quotes or provocative questions to decorate the room. Skip the environmentally unkind foam boards and easel rentals, and just print hangable digital banners with non-damaging removeable wall strips.

AUDIO/VISUAL

- *Share.* If appropriate from a health and safety perspective, save some money by having the panelists share microphones. Yes, they will all want their own, but sharing actually creates a sense of collaboration and a desire to balance the airtime between panelists.

- *Delete.* In a room of less than 50 people, you can get by without a dedicated microphone for audience Q&A, 50 to 75 depends on the acoustics of the room, over 75 a microphone is mandatory so the audience can hear the question. In any case, be sure to have audience microphone runners.

39 RETHINK YOUR SEATING PLAN

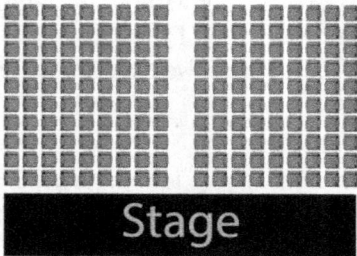

You walk into a room and see a traditional seating setup for your panel discussion: Long draped table at the front on a raised stage, theater-style with two columns of chairs, a path down the middle. The screen is at the front in the middle of the room. Looks pretty good, right?

While typical for many meeting venues, and perhaps most comfortable for you, the presenter, meeting organizer, or hotelier, it is *not* the best seating arrangement for an audience-centered discussion.

So what's wrong with straight rows?

FOCUS. The seats directly in front of the speakers are the only decent seats in the house. Everyone else has to adjust their view to get a direct line of sight to the moderator and panelists. And yet we give up this prime real estate to a multimedia projector table or vacant space for a center aisle. Whenever possible, place the chairs in front of the panel for:

ENERGY. Any feng-shui expert will tell you that the energy flows out of a room through a center aisle. Wherever possible, keep the straight row center section right in front of you, with an aisle in between each outer seating section.

SAFETY You may want to have some ability for people to get in and out of their seats, so you can modify the seating with some extra aisles starting a third of the way from the stage. This way, the energy won't flow out of the room.

BLOCKED VIEW. Unless you are sitting in the front row, there will always be somebody taller or wider in the seat in front of you. If you're lucky, you'll have a semi-obstructed view. Worst case, you have to lean just to get a clear view. Wherever possible, stagger the chairs so they aren't lined up like soldiers behind each other.

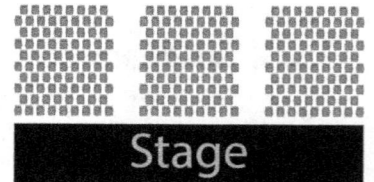

PAIN. Unless you're sitting right in front of the speakers, chances are you must turn your neck slightly to see the moderator and panelists. If you're on the far reaches, then you're probably putting more weight on one butt cheek than the other and are constantly readjusting your seat. Do this for an extended period of time, and it starts to hurt. Wherever possible, angle the chairs toward the front.

DISCONNECT. If you want to connect with the audience, enable the audience to connect with each other. They simply can't connect with each other if they can't see each other. Straight rows allow each person in the row to see only one person on either side (and the back of somebody's head—but that doesn't help connection!) Wherever possible, curve the seating around the stage area so the audience can see each other. If space allows, consider having the audience sit in table rounds to encourage discussion.

PANEL-IN-THE-ROUND 40

You walk into the convention ballroom and immediately recognize that this meeting is going to be different. The stage is not at the front of the room, but in the middle of the room. There is no lectern—no front to the stage! The chairs are placed closely around all sides of the stage, with highboy tables lining the back ring of chairs. There are four screens hanging from the rafters, much like a jumbotron in an athletic stadium.

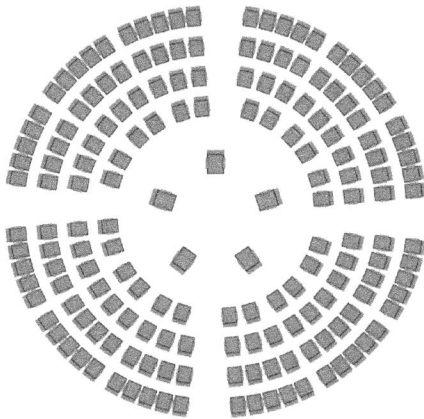

Oh yeah. This is not the typical meeting room set.

Welcome to the most intimate seating arrangement for a large group: Theater-in-the-round. It's an audience-centric room set where the audience is looking at each other during the meeting, making deeper connections with each other and with the speakers. It also allows more engagement and involvement with the audience since 50% of the audience is closer to the stage than typical theater-style seating.

Theater-in-the-round is not all that new. Common in Greek and Roman times, (remember the Coliseum?), theater in the round is used worldwide for small, intimate plays and performances. But for large events? Is this even possible?

Sarah Michel, VP at Velvet Chainsaw Consulting, has staged several of these style events. She responds, "Absolutely! The goal is to bring the audience into the conversation, to create connections and enthusiasm for the meeting. You can't do that in a traditional format with hundreds of people, but you can in a theater-in-the-round."

To do panel-in-the-round style (otherwise known as a fishbowl format), consider these key factors:

- Select a venue and A/V crew that will work with this unique seating arrangement. Check references as they may say they have done it, but they might not.

- The stage is always in the center and can be rectangular, circular, diamond, or triangular. The stage is usually on an even level with the audience, on risers, or below the audience in a pit formation. For high-end meetings, you can even have the stage set on a slow rotation turntable that makes a rotation every 15 minutes. That's slow enough to minimize disruption to the presenters and fast enough that everyone has a chance to maintain eye contact. *Note: If on a riser, it's smart to have two sets of stairs for the presenters to get to the stage.*

- Any furniture and scenery should not obscure the stage or inhibit the audience from seeing. Generally, less is better.

- As with all meetings, you want to make sure the center stage is well-lit since the panelists should be visible from all sides without blinding nearby audience members. You may need to rig some drop down lights or keep the ballroom lights up.

- The chairs should be placed as close to the stage as possible, staggered so each person is looking *between* the heads of the two people sitting in front of them.

- If the budget allows, the jumbotron idea is great to display video images of the panelists (and their slides, if any). Otherwise, set two to four projection screens on the outer walls.

- Last, but not least, are your panelists. Most have never spoken in the round, so you'll need to give them advanced coaching. It's not the same as speaking to an audience from a main stage.

41 THE PERFECT CHAIRS

I stumbled upon a picture of a panel recently and cringed. The moderator and panelists were sitting on simple, 4 legged barstools with an itty bitty circular seat. They looked extremely uncomfortable and I can't imagine it made for stimulating conversation.

So what makes the perfect chair to incite an interesting and impact-full discussion of ideas?

It certainly isn't the standard hotel chair behind a white draped table. Nor is it the big, high back stuffed chair better suited to a living room that no one uses. While they may look nice, your panelists don't know how to sit in them. Should they sit back into the chair, they look like a slouch. If they sit forward (which I recommend), then they can't use the back of the chair for comfort. And because the seat is typically so big, do they sit on the right or the left side of the seat? And, if short in stature, it looks odd when their feet can't touch the ground. The second cousin to the high back dining room chair is a typical dining room chair. These are more comfortable and you can space them closer to each other, creating a more intimate setting. Keep in mind, unless you have the panelists up on a platform or riser, then the participants in the back may not be able to see what's going on.

My preference? I like a tall (bar-height), well-made, and sturdy director's chair or barstool—the Goldilocks of chairs: not too small, not too big, but just right! A barstool/director's chair adds an element of informality and a conversational tone to the room. The shape of the chair almost forces the panelists to sit forward and engage. Make sure the chairs do NOT swivel and DO have a sturdy footrest.

Arrange the chairs in a shallow semi-circle with a small cocktail table to the side for notes and water. Make it extra special by embroidering the back with the conference logo or panelists' names. As an extra special surprise and thank you, I ship the personalized chair to each panelist after the event.

It's also a wise idea to let the panelists know beforehand what kind of chairs you're using. They are probably expecting a traditional setup and might rethink wearing a short skirt, holey (or no) socks, and other potential wardrobe malfunctions once they know they won't be hidden behind a draped table.

Cozier and more comfortable furniture creates a more intimate and interesting dialogue.

THE MODERATOR STATION 42

I'm often asked where the moderator should be. There's no standard spot, make your decision based on the pros and cons of each option:

STANDING AT A LECTERN. Although you have a place to put your notes, the lectern is a barrier between you and everyone else.

STAND TO THE SIDE. The moderator stands stage right and is free to move about the stage. It may be harder to get eye contact and intervene with the panelists when standing on the side, but you can use movement to your advantage.

SEATED AMONG THE PANELISTS. The moderator sits (rather than stands) stage right. Again, it can be difficult to intervene.

SEATED BETWEEN THE PANELISTS. Perfect for a debate format, this style enables you to intervene easily in either direction. It also makes you the focal point for the audience, splits the panel in half and makes it harder for panelists to interact with each other.

IN THE AUDIENCE. Often referred to as Oprah-style, this style makes you the center of attention. It's best when there are significant audience questions and interaction.

My personal preference is to start on the side for the introductory remarks, and then move into the audience. Panelists tend to talk to the moderator, so when you move into the audience, it appears that the panelists are talking to them. And it gives me more latitude to change up the format when needed.

43 MICROPHONES

For audiences under 30 people, you may not require microphones. Between 30–50, it's nice to have. Over 50, use some kind of amplification system. Even if you don't think you need it, other people will appreciate it.

If your budget allows, the moderator and each panelist should have a headset, lavaliere, or handheld microphone. If working with a modest budget, share a cordless handheld among two panelists. (So if you have four panelists, then you'll need two microphones plus one for the moderator.)

The **MODERATOR** should *always* have a dedicated microphone—the type is dependent on their preference. The moderator can use the lectern microphone, a wireless handheld or lavaliere microphone. If moving into the audience for Q&A, the moderator will need (at least) a wireless handheld to capture audience comments. I prefer to use a Samson E-50 headset that plugs into the lavaliere pack. The audio is fabulous and the Samson has three different plugs (Shure, Audio-Technica and Sennheiser) so it will plug into just about any professional sound system. And it has a little band behind the ear so it doesn't fall off.

Each **PANELIST** should have an individual wireless handheld, lavaliere or headset microphone; however, budget or logistics may make it necessary to share between two or even three panelists. When sharing a microphone, a wireless handheld is preferable. If sitting at a table, a table microphone is acceptable.

You may need to have microphones in the **AUDIENCE** as well. If the moderator stays on the stage, have a runner (or two) with a wireless microphone in hand or a wireless or corded microphone on a stand in strategic places throughout the audience. You may also want to experiment with a throwable microphone (try Catchbox) or activate your smartphones (CrowdMics.com) to capture audience comments.

Make sure you sweet talk the A/V tech ahead of time and not only do a sound check, but a sound level for yourself and each panelist. Find out how the tech is going to adjust the sound levels. My preference is to keep the microphones hot throughout the panel discussion and only mute a panelist if they start coughing, wheezing or for other audio burbles. Finally, advise your panelists to speak with energy into the microphone.

Most panelists use their built-in computer microphones, however if you want to create an outstanding audio experience for the listeners, then encourage them to use a good, external microphone. I use a Yeti Nano with a touch button to mute and unmute my microphone.

For quality control, consider sending the panelists a kit that includes the appropriate lights, camera, and microphone.

MICROPHONE RUNNER RULES 44

Being a microphone runner is more complex than just handing a person a microphone and saying, "Go find me some questions." As a moderator, train your microphone runners to effectively solicit questions from the audience and know both roles:

KNOW THY MICROPHONE. The A/V team will give you a cordless microphone that probably has a piece of tape with the microphone number written on it. That's your number and your microphone. Have them show you how to turn it on and off. Typically, the A/V team will hand you the microphone right before the panel *already turned on.* You don't have to do anything. If need be, the A/V team will mute your microphone from the main soundboard.

CONSTANTLY SCAN. Look around your designated section of the audience for the next questioner. For larger audiences with multiple runners, you'll divide the room up into segments: You have this half of the room; your mic runner buddy will have the other half. Your responsibility is to cover your designated section. You'll want to have an aisle seat in your section so you can be ready for the Q&A.

SIGNAL INTEREST. As you walk down the aisle, hold the microphone out to the audience, showing your interest in identifying the next questioner. During the Q&A session, start at the front of your section, face the audience (your back will be to the stage) and walk down the aisle, looking for the next question. Don't be shy about showing people you're holding a microphone, but don't be obnoxious, either.

RUN TO THE QUESTIONER. Stand by their side and raise your hand high so the moderator knows where you are. When someone indicates interest, run over to them. That's why you are called the mic runner. (Ladies, this is a good time to mention it is much more comfortable to run in flat shoes. You don't have to wear your marathon running shoes, but a comfortable shoe that allows you to dash around a ballroom.)

STAND TALL. SMILE. BE KIND. Be reassuring until it is their turn to talk. You may have to stand there for a while because the moderator will typically go in sequence between mic runners. While waiting, be positive. Send good wishes in their direction. Sounds kinda *woo-woo* but there is a distinct difference in the questions posed from a grumpy vs. happy mic runner.

NEVER GIVE UP THE MICROPHONE. In my experience, the moment you hand the questioner the microphone, you have just given license for that person to give a speech—even if the moderator provided specific instructions on how the Q&A session should go. To keep the questions tight and succinct, hold on to the microphone. Even so, sometimes that's not as important or the meeting organizer would prefer the questioner takes the microphone. In that case, I suggest you bend the knee or take an open seat while the person asks their question. In this way, you are not in the way of other attendees or the camera.

HOLD THE MICROPHONE A FIST AWAY from the questioner's mouth. The average person doesn't know how to hold a microphone. If you hand it to them, they'll fiddle with the on/off switch, ask if you can hear them, and hold the microphone too far away for adequate projection. The optimal placement of the head of the microphone is about a fist away from the person's mouth. That's actually closer than most think!

STAY BY THEIR SIDE. Stand next to the person until the question has been understood by the panel, then go in search of the next questioner. After the person asks the question, the panel might have a clarifying question, so you don't want to leave their side too soon but you do want to find the next questioner. If it's just you, you need to hoof it. If there are two runners, you'll have a bit more time. With three runners, you'll have even more.

WHEN READY WITH THE NEXT QUESTIONER, raise your hand high so the moderator knows where you are. The key here is that there's no lag time between questions. The panel finishes one question, the moderator immediately sees a runner with a hand up and the next question starts. Depending on the room set up, sometimes the stage lights are so bright it will be hard for the moderator to see you. So knowing that it is your turn, you may want to do a simple shout of "Here!" so the moderator knows where you are.

ENJOY YOURSELF. If you have fun, they will too! Don't be grumpy, bored, or lethargic; the audience will pick up on your lackluster attitude and won't volunteer. Instead, be lively, interested, and energetic, and they will be as well.

> Obviously, you won't use a microphone runner in the virtual world, but you can use an ombudsman or technician who mutes and unmutes the microphones, recognizes the raising of hands, and rummages through the chatbox for the best questions to ask.

USING A THROWABLE MICROPHONE

I'm a HUGE fan of Catchbox, a throwable microphone that I use (almost) all the time for audience Q&A during interviews and panel discussions. Perfect for groups over 75 (or where a microphone is needed) and less than 300. For larger audiences, I recommend several Catchboxes—one per 300 is a nice ratio.

I use the Catchbox because it:

IS NOVEL. Audiences like new things—especially techie audiences who love gadgets. It adds a bit of excitement and variety.

IS A TIME-SAVER. In the past, I would be running around the room with a cordless handheld. There would be a few seconds lost between getting from one questioner to the next—who might very well be on the other side of the room.

ENGAGES THE AUDIENCE. Even if you are not throwing or catching the Catchbox, it's always fun to see objects fly around the room! Applaud for a great throw or catch! Howl when the Catchbox hits someone on the head! (Yes, that does happen from time to time, but not very often.)

GIVES THE AUDIENCE POWER. Rather than have the questioner throw the Catchbox back to me, I have the questioner select the next person to throw it to. Sometimes, it's a simple hand off to a neighbor, a Hail Mary pass to the other side of the room, or something in between. The key is that the audience gets to choose.

However, there is one downfall. For years I would fervently hang onto the cordless microphone in fear a questioner would try to grab it from me—especially when I knew there might be a speech coming. My thought was that when you give up the microphone, you give up control.

With Catchbox, you give up control of the microphone. The audience is in control. *Egads!*

All is not lost. There are two specific actions you can take to keep control:

1. **INTRODUCE CATCHBOX.** When you first bring out the Catchbox:

   - *Explain How It Works.* Show the audience how to speak into it. Throw it to a few people and ask them to comment "Wow! That's light!"

   - *Set Ground Rules.* You know what could go wrong, so set some rules up front. I like to say, "We have a fairly tight time frame, so we would all appreciate it if you keep your questions short and to the point. We don't have time for a lengthy speech. Please ask your question, then give a sentence of background or amplifying information, when you're done, YOU get to choose who will get the Catchbox next! You can throw it anywhere in the room. I just ask that you keep the Catchbox moving all around the room" and I use a grand gesture to signify the Catchbox going all over.

   - *Ask For the First Question.* Rather than saying, "Are there any questions?" assume that the audience has questions and ask, "Who has the first question?" If you're really nervous about this, you may want to have a friend in the audience ready to ask an interesting question.

2. **INTERVENE QUICKLY.** Now that you have the ground rules in place, you can intervene fairly quickly to refocus a questioner. Of course, this is directly dependent on your facilitation style. Mine is pretty direct and to the point. Here's how I've handled some rebels:

    - If the questioner starts to make a speech, I'll interrupt and ask, "So what's the question?" Yes, they'll get a little off-balance and think you're being persnickety, but the rest of the audience knows what you're doing and is supremely grateful. The rest of the questioners will fall in line.

    - If the questioner is using more than two sentences to explain, interject, "Only one more sentence, please" or "Wrap it up, please." If they go into a speech, say, "Please, no speeches. We don't have time."

    - If Catchbox has been hanging out at one part of the room, provide a little coaching by saying, "Catchbox has been hanging out with you folks for a while. How 'bout we move toward this side of the room? They'd like to ask some questions too."

When you introduce Catchbox with confidence and ground rules, you can intervene quickly to keep the Q&A focused, energized, lively and fun.

PART TWO

MODERATE

A

PANEL DISCUSSION

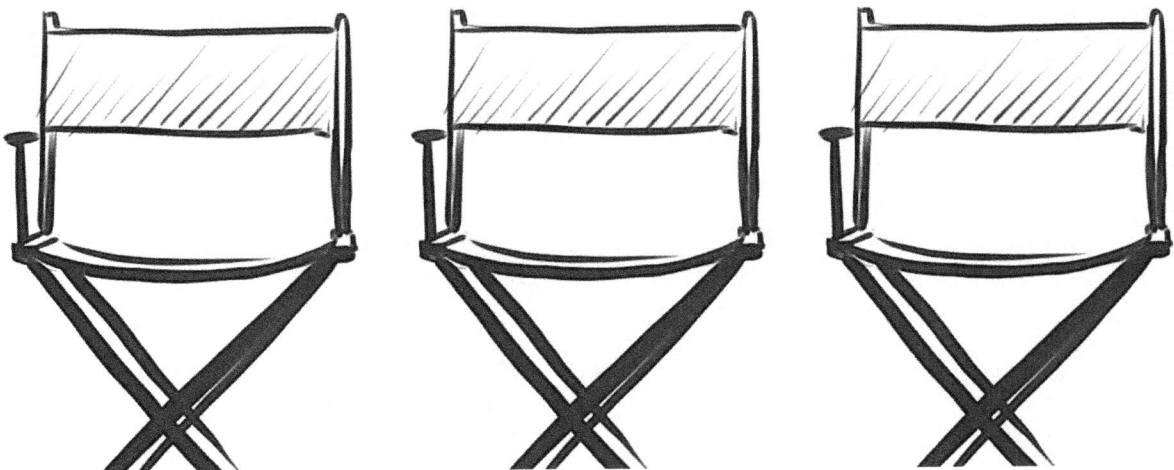

CHAPTER SIX
OPEN WITH PIZAZZ!

Grab the attention of the audience with a relevant fact, statistic, quotation, anecdote or joke. Then welcome the audience, thank panelists, link the opening line to the purpose of the panel, and preview how the panel will unfold. Be explicit about when and how audience members can ask questions. The opening sets the tone for the entire panel; carefully craft and rehearse it until your delivery is smooth and enthusiastic.

~ Christine Clapp

THE FIRST FEW MINUTES of your panel discussion are absolutely critical. Although people shouldn't judge a book by its cover, they do. While every audience has a different personality, they all want to know they're in good hands; they need to know you care about them and they can trust you to deliver.

After all, you've done your homework. You have a solid process in place. You know the panelists. They are prepared and now it is Showtime!

Take one or two minutes to warmly welcome the audience and solidify your connection. Tee up the topic. Tell them what they can expect as a result of investing time with you and the panelists.

And for goodness sakes, do NOT give a speech. Do NOT start with a story about yourself, prattle on about how honored you are to moderate the panel, regale us with all your knowledge about the topic. I hate to break this to you, but no one cares what your problems are. They care about what the panel is going to impart to make their lives better.

Depending on your comfort level, select a technique from this chapter (or a combination of techniques) and adjust it to work with your panel topic.

THE FIVE OPENING ELEMENTS

The opening segment typically consists of five distinct elements. Each element has a specific purpose that may be accomplished at the beginning or in program materials.

1. **TOPIC INTRODUCTION.** Welcome the audience and lead into the topic with a short, interesting hook that grabs their attention. DO NOT repeat verbatim what is in the program. Give it a fresh spin that rephrases and focuses on the promise.

2. **YOUR ROLE.** Take just a few moments to state your name, your affiliation, your qualifications to moderate the panel and a short definition of your role as moderator—30 seconds, TOPS.

3. **AGENDA AND PROCESS.** Let the audience know what's going to be covered, general guidelines about the process, ground rules, timing, and when and where to direct questions.

4. **HOUSEKEEPING.** There may be some announcements that need to be made, depending on your unique circumstances:

   - *Handout Availability.* "There should be a handout for each participant as you walked in the door" or "These slides will be posted on SlideShare.net or the organization's website tomorrow."

   - *Recording Instructions.* "This presentation is being recorded so if you are asking a question, please step forward to a microphone." Or "If you don't want to be videotaped for this panel discussion, I suggest you sit on the left side of the room—out of the view of the camera."

   - *Breaks.* For long panel formats, provide a break schedule.

   - *Phones.* Tell the audience to silence their cell phones, tweet with a specific hashtag, take pictures, or other reminders they may need.

5. **PANELIST INTRODUCTIONS.** Regardless of whether you're doing the introducing or they are introducing themselves, you set the process in place. Remember, the whole point of doing introductions is to connect the audience with the panelists; who they may or may not know.

Depending on your situation, you may do all or just a few of these opening elements. It's your call. When you confidently start your panel discussion, you'll set the panelists up for success and let the audience know they are in good hands.

> Depending on the familiarity of the audience with the technology, you may want to give a quick tutorial on some of the basic features: As people join, ask how familiar they are with the digital platform. Give them a quick walk through of the features.

START FAST, GIVE HOPE 45

The problem: Most panels start with an incredibly long, incomprehensible, multi-part question directed to the first panelist. The person starts talking and she's going to keep speaking until she's done.

It might be possible to salvage the conversation, however, the vast majority of moderators hot potato the question to panelist #2 for an opinion. Of course, they'll answer the multi-part question. And how long are they going to speak? The exact length that panelist #1 talked, of course! Otherwise, they'll feel they aren't providing as much value as panelist #1. So they go on and on without adding much to the conversation.

It gets worse. The moderator looks at panelist #3, who is sending the visual signal of "Of course you're going to ask me." And what does the moderator say? "Now for, panelist #3, what do you think?"

And then panelist #3 offers their opinion. What? Is this answer going to be short? No! That's impossible because two speakers have already gone on and on and on and on. So panelist #3 will keep going the exact length that panelists #1 and #2 took, while adding no additional content.

What if there are four panelists? Even though the moderator might sense that *perhaps* something has gone awry, how can you not ask the fourth panelist? Who does nothing but recap everything the prior panelists said, and will keep going until at long last, they are all done.

The problem is that this first question has gone on for 20 minutes and the audience has completely checked out. They're doing the math: "We heard one question that took 20 minutes. How many questions are we going to get to in this 60-minute panel?" And at that moment, you can see it in their eyes. They have given up hope. They start wondering, *how close am I to the door? Can I make a quick exit?*

This is not how to do it.

You actually want to start fast and give them hope.

According to Brian Walter, founder of Extreme Meetings, you want to "Ask a slightly less complex question and then you, as the moderator, are poised like a panther on a branch, waiting for a baby deer to walk by. You're ready to pounce the second that there is a pause and you're going to interject more of a follow-up question. And after that, you're going to immediately go for a contrast with someone else on the panel."

Check out the example on the next page:

Here's an example:

BRIAN: Connie what's the biggest financial mistake most speakers make during their first five years?

CONNIE: They fall for the myth that there's going to be tons of exposure, so they agreed to do something for free.

BRIAN: Really now, why is that? Why do they do that?

CONNIE: Because they're desperate and they believe people are nice and they're going to get hired.

BRIAN: Interesting. Tammy do you agree with Connie? You think she's crazy? What do you think?

TAMMY: Separate questions but I disagree because I think when you're getting started, you should speak as often as you can to get yourself on the stage so you get better and better as a speaker.

BRIAN: Interesting. Sylvie, who's right? Connie or Tammy?

SYLVIE: Neither of them. Neither is right because it always depends. It depends on the situation you're in, your business. Do you need exposure or not? I think it depends.

BRIAN: David, settle this. Who's crazy? Who's right?

DAVID: Well, I think you know speakers who don't like to sell. I always say I'd rather be salesy than brokey!

WOW! How much time did that take? 52 seconds, five questions, four panelists weighed in with four different opinions. In one minute, we've given the audience hope. They're now thinking, 'That was fast moving. I wonder if it's going to be like this the entire time?'

Here's a final hint from Walter: "Start fast and show that you will interject quickly when there's a micro-pause when it seems that the panelist has finished her question. Now, if Connie had said 'and…' and I cut her off, you would say 'Gosh, that guy is rude.' So, you have to make sure a thought gets finished before you jump in, but jump in you must!"

It all hinges on that first question and answer. It could destroy your entire discussion; it's tough to recover. Why not start fast to give hope?

ASK PROVOCATIVE QUESTIONS 46

A panel without some kind of controversy, otherwise known as a difference of opinion, results in an extremely boring panel.

So start with a bang; ask an interesting, intriguing, provocative or polarizing question to stimulate discourse.

You can ask the same *provocative* question to all the panelists. For example, "What's the absolute, biggest challenge related to our topic?" or, "What's the one thing you did that made you successful in this topic?" or, "If you could go back in time, what would be the one thing you would do differently?"

Or, you can target a unique *polarizing* question to each panelist to give a unique point of view that each panelist is well-qualified to talk about. For example, "Expert A (could be a panelist, but doesn't have to be) says [this] about [the topic]. Do you agree or disagree and why?"

Author and panel moderator Scott Berkun shares this example: "Will blogging still be here in the year 2022? Assign each panelist a yes or no end of that question. If they balk at this being artificial, ask them to propose a better question, or series of questions to frame the debate. Pick the right spine and many problems will take care of themselves."

You can even ask the audience a provocative or polarizing question:

- As a rhetorical question, without asking for answers.
- As a direct question, while taking a poll.
- As a direct question, soliciting a few responses from the audience.
- As a question to be discussed in small groups.

When you start with a controversial question at the beginning of a panel discussion, your audience will lean in to learn more.

47 POLL THE AUDIENCE

An easy way to start a panel discussion is for the panel moderator to poll the audience for three specific reasons:

1. To get a baseline for who is in the room and discover commonalities among participants.
2. To gain an appreciation for what the audience wants the panelists to talk about.
3. To create the expectation that the audience will be further involved in the discussion.

You can poll the audience a number of ways:

SHOW OF HANDS. Ask those who agree with your question to raise their hands.

ROUND-ROBIN. With a small audience, go around the room and ask each person to state their position.

THUMBS. Have those who agree with the point you just made show you a thumbs-up and those who don't a thumbs-down. A sideways thumb can mean undecided.

STAND UP. Ask those in agreement or who find the statement to be true to stand up. Those who disagree or find your statement to be false can remain seated.

NOISE. Clap to agree and stomp to disagree. Or, if confidentiality is important, ask those who agree to hum. You'll find those who are passionate will hum loudly.

SHOUT. Say "Of course!" if you agree and "No way!" if you don't. The volume can also show the strength of the person's commitment.

SCALE FROM 1 TO 10. Ask the audience to shout out their number—on a scale from 1 to 10 where 1 is low and 10 is high (or other opposing attributes). The resulting cacophony can show how far or close the group is to agreement.

RESPONSE CARDS. Ask participants to select and hold up the appropriate color-coded card/paper that signifies their response. These are ideal for multiple-choice and true-false questions or those with a range of responses (agree/neutral/disagree; high/medium/low).

WAVE YOUR FLAG. Similar to response cards, ask the audience to wave a color flag that signifies their response. Try using green for agree, yellow for neutral or have some concerns, and red for disagree.

CONTINUUM. Have one side of the room take one stance (definitely) and the other side the polar opposite (no way!), or think of your own clever scale (vested to don't care).

ELECTRONIC POLLING. Many moderators use PollEverywhere.com, but if you're using it for an audience larger than 40 people, there is a fee. I use Slido.com where you can create an event in less than a minute. Participants use one simple link to join in using their smart phones, ask questions, and vote for their favorite. You can even moderate the questions to remove the junk like "hi mom!" or take a poll on the fly in the middle of the session.

HOW TO TAKE A POLL

STEP 1   **ASK THE QUESTION**

Ask your well thought-out question and model the behavior you want to see. For example, "Who here...?" and while you're asking the question, raise your hand high in the air, waive your green flag, or stomp your foot. This sends a clear signal that you're expecting the audience who agree to perform that behavior with you.

STEP 2   **REPORT THE RESULT**

You may be the only person in the room who can see all the results, and inquiring minds want to know. Share the results in the form of a statistic: "That looks like 30 folks, so that's 10% of the group." (Want to make it a tad bit funny? Report out the numbers in a precise way, even though it's obviously a best guesstimate. For example, you could say "Twenty-seven folks agree, and that is 13.3% of the group.")

STEP 3   **OPTIONAL FOLLOW UP**

You can also ask some additional questions to a couple of people near you to get the conversation going.

Particularly with virtual panels, only take a poll when you want to know the answer. Otherwise, ask a rhetorical question for audience consideration/self-reflection and move on.

Your digital platform will have a polling feature.
You must either frontload the poll or create an instant poll.
However, depending on the size of the group, let your imagination run
with different, creative ways to take a poll.

Some ideas include:
Literally raise your hand if everyone is showing video
Raise a colored object that shows your choice
Use the "raise hand" functionality
Use your emotion buttons (thumbs up or clap hands)
Comment in the chatbox
Turn your sound on and make a noise

48 SWITCH! AN IMPROV OPENING

In improv comedy, the first rule is AGREE. Always agree and say "Yes", never say "No". When you're improvising, this means you're required to agree with whatever your partner has created then add something to the conversation.

For a lively start to your panel discussion, take a cue from improv comedy where the plot, characters, and dialogue of a scene are made up in the moment. Start with a provocative question to the panelists while explaining to the audience you will be using an improv technique called "Yes and…" for the panelists to answer.

Direct your question to the first panelist. After five seconds or so, ring a bell, shout to switch or send some other signal for the next panelist to continue the thread. Panelist #2 then talks for about five seconds or so until you send the signal again.

This is a great technique to use to when you have many panelists on stage and want to get them all involved quickly.

> Because the panelists are not literally sitting next to each other,
> they will not know the order of the lineup unless you tell them.
> Ask them to keep their microphones on and tell them their lineup.
> Repeat the question and let the improv begin.
> Don't be surprised if you have to cue the next person to talk
> by simply stating their first name.

TELL AN INTERESTING STORY 49

Once upon a time…

What happened to you physically as you read those words? If you are like most people, you exhaled and you released the tension in your shoulders as you prepared to listen to a story.

Stories create a quintessential bonding experience between moderator, panelists, and audience. Next time you're at a panel or presentation, watch how a simple story can bring an audience to life. You can actually see a visible change when you or the panelists tell a story that humanizes and personalizes your topic. Most participants will lean forward, smile, and either nod or shake their heads.

When listeners hear a well-told story, they take a journey with you, correlating their own experiences with yours. Your story becomes their story—or it reminds them of a very similar story from their own lives. Think of it this way: We all have a figurative file drawer that contains all of the information we know. And it's easier to take in *new* information when we can relate it to something that resides in that file drawer.

At the very onset, consider sharing a story that connects to the topic and sparks interest in the audience. Share the impact (benefits as well as unfavorable consequences) of your topic on the reality of their lives if the present situation is or is not resolved. Don't forget to choose descriptive words using the names of actual persons, places, or events and give your story an ample sprinkling of color and life.

My favorite types of stories for panels are comparisons, contrasts, allusions, and analogies.

COMPARISONS show similarities whereas **CONTRASTS** show differences. Common comparisons and contrasts include:

- Is/is not.
- Retrospective/prospective. (That was then; this is now.)
- Point/counterpoint.
- Review/preview.

ALLUSIONS occur when you are making brief, indirect references to a person, place, or event that everybody can identify. An allusion evokes a connection among three parties—you, the audience, and the image you are referencing—without saying who, what, or where it is.

Let's look at a few categories you can allude to in order to get your audience exploring rather than snoring:

- *Politicians.* Politicians are famous for serving up some phrases that stick. By mentioning the well-known phrase, there is a connection to that time and place in history. For example, "Ask not what your country can do for you, but what you can do for your country" evokes the memory of John F. Kennedy.
- *Current events.* You can allude to a current event at a local, regional, or national level. You can also tap into what is happening among the participants' organizations if that information is widely known.
- *Celebrities.* Some celebrities have enduring personalities. They may not be endearing, but they are well-known and thus worthy targets of allusion, even after they are long gone. When I am introduced, my special wave to wordlessly say hello to the audience is an allusion to Princess Diana.
- *Flashback.* Refer to something said earlier in the presentation or conference.

AN ANALOGY is a comparison of two things to highlight some strong point(s) they have in common. Analogies are often used in technical panel discussions as a way to connect the unknown (what you are presenting) to something the audience already knows. There are basically two ways we express an analogy:

- *A simile* compares two things that are not the same and not normally considered together. The key words you'll use when using a simile are "like" or "as." For example, your brain is like a computer. As you read this book, your brain is storing information just as your computer stores data.
- *A metaphor* is a more direct version of a simile that talks about one thing as if it is the other. Take out the "like" or "as" and your simile becomes a metaphor.

Finding just the right analogy to kick off your panel discussion can be a challenge.

HOW TO SELECT AN ANALOGY

My colleague, Betsy Allen shared four steps for selecting an analogy.

STEP 1   CLARIFY THE PURPOSE AND PEOPLE
First, clarify your target and the outcome you are after. I oversaw the Welfare to Work Training in Lee County, Florida, and helped boat builders in Fort Myers tap federal funding to put new wage earners to work as fiberglass handlers. My audience was primarily minority females who had probably never been on a boat much less knew anything about building one! Yet, within 25 hours, we needed them to know every step of building a boat, and we needed a visual memory hook that would stay top of mind as they became independent workers.

STEP 2   DEFINE THE ELEMENTS, PIECES, OR PARTS
Fiberglass handling is messy work. It's done outdoors in the heat of summer, with hazardous chemicals and challenging conditions. The process uses wet (resin) and dry (reinforcement) ingredients that are temperamental. When used out of sequence or measured inaccurately, the combinations can start fires. In fact, if you do everything right, yet don't have the fiberglass rubbed out within 30 minutes, you have to start over.

STEP 3   BRAINSTORM SIMILES AND METAPHORS
Analogies are everywhere. After brainstorming metaphors that were visual and could be connected to the audience and purpose, we landed on: Building a boat is like baking a cake.

STEP 4   NARROW THE POTENTIALS THAT LINK BACK TO YOUR PURPOSE
You bake a cake from the inside out, just as you build a boat. You have wet and dry ingredients, which must be accurately measured and baked delicately to create a cake. The same holds true for a boat. Finally, the last step of the process is to rub out the fiberglass before it hardens just as you rub on the frosting while it's soft.

Selecting your analogy is more of an art than a science; it takes a bit of thought to pick just the right one to kick off your panel discussion.

MAKE AN OBSERVATION 50

Personally, I'm not a big fan of telling jokes, but anyone can make a humorous observation about the topic or the panelists.

Here are some idea starters for you:

- Share something interesting and complimentary about the panelists.
- Share the impact (good and bad).
- Offer a direct-to-the-heart-of-the-matter statement linking everyone in the room to the topic.
- Share a recent occurrence or success story related to the topic.

For example, my all-time favorite comes from Mark Sanborn who made an observation that set the tone for the discussion while connecting the panelists (the CEOs of California Pizza Kitchen, Cinnabon, and Forbes) in a humorous way:

"As I was preparing for this program, I just finished lunch at California Pizza Kitchen, where I eat every week... I grabbed a Cinnabon, which is my favorite dessert...as I was reading my Forbes magazine which I've subscribed to since I was twelve, and I remember thinking, how can I begin this panel without seeming patronizing?"

His introduction received a huge laugh from the audience.

Moreover, it kept the panelists from feeling like they had to hawk their products—because Mark just did it for them.

51 SHARE FUN FACTS OR STATISTICS

One of my favorite TV characters is Cliff Claven from *Cheers*, a quirky postman who knew scads of meaningless trivia. He would say, "It's a little known fact..." followed by a pithy factoid. You, too, can open with pizazz using an unusual, striking, startling or surprising fact or statistic that hooks the audience into the topic.

What kind of facts? Here's a potential list to get you started, although you'll need to do a bit of research to find these nuggets:

- *Topic.* Serve up some interesting facts about your topic as a "Did you know...?" or "Ever wonder why...?"

- *Audience.* During your prework, you might have stumbled upon an interesting bit of trivia about a particular person in the group or the entire group.

- *Location.* Present some interesting facts about the venue or city that relate to your message.

- *Benefits.* Is there an interesting fact about the people who will benefit from your call to action that would be of interest to your listeners?

- *Process.* Is there something unique about how your topic is going to be accomplished?

- *Benchmarks.* Has someone else conducted an analysis of the topic that would be noteworthy to share?

- *Current Event.* What is going on in the community, city, state, nation, or world that is interesting to your listeners? Check the morning newspaper, a professional journal, or a local news program and link something that has recently made the news with the topic or within the industry.

- *History.* What happened in history on the specific date of the panel discussion? Connect it to the meeting theme or the panelists.

When it comes to statistics, create a way to make the statistic come to life and have meaning for the audience, emphasizing the truly important part of the fact, statistic, or trend.

- *Put the Number in a Day-to-Day Context.* Compare your statistic with some other well-known fact that can be easily understood by the audience. For example, you could say "According to a study released by the National Center for Educational Statistics, 43 million American adults are functionally illiterate. 21%. That means one in five of us is unable to read well enough to do our jobs, lead fulfilling lives, or even read a presentation handout."

- *Illustrate the Statistic.* In order for your audience to understand and visualize the enormity of the statistic, use visual images. Describe something as "the equivalent of two football fields end to end" so people can literally see the numbers and the length in their mind's eye.

- *Be Precise.* Round off the data if you want the audience to comprehend the number quickly; be more precise if you want to add to the believability of the statistic. Your audience may well forget the actual number you give, but they will easily remember the picture.

- *Be Specific.* Beware of using the phrase "Many authorities declare…" Your audience will wonder who the authorities are and Google your facts during the panel discussion. Be specific and name the source(s). Understand where and how the data was generated—just in case you get a question from the audience.

FACT OR FICTION 52

Before the event, preselect some statements about the topic that not everyone in the audience knows—or where there might be some disagreement. You can obtain these statements from the panelists, the meeting organizer, or participants themselves through social media or interviews.

Share the statement with the audience and then take a poll as to whether it is a fact or fiction.

For example, "All panels need a panel moderator. Fact or Fiction?"

You can ask each table to discuss whether it is a fact or fiction and why. Or you can ask each audience member to wave a flag to indicate their opinion, (green for agree, red for disagree, yellow for undecided).

The panel moderator takes a bird's eye view of the poll and shares the results. "Looks like 90% of you agree the statement is true. A few are undecided and a few more don't agree at all."

The panel then shares their answers and opinions for about two minutes. I typically ask the panelist who submitted the statement to start the discussion. If it came from me or an unidentified source, I'll just call on whoever looks ready to respond.

Similar to taking a poll, this technique is an either/or proposition.
You either think it is true or false. Fact or Crap. Agree or Disagree.
It's much easier to get the audience to answer in the chatbox,
shout at their monitor or raise their hands.
If the question is seminal to the panel discussion,
move into breakout groups; otherwise,
skip the breakouts since it takes a bit more time.

53 PLAY THE NEWLYWED GAME

Remember the Newlywed Game where one newlywed would answer a question on a large poster board and their partner would have to guess what it was? You can do a similar opening activity by giving each panelist a fat, black marker and stiff poster board.

After you've introduced the panelists, ask a pointed, provocative question directly related to the topic such as, "In one word, what drives you crazy about this topic?" or "What's the biggest benefit to this topic?" While they are writing their answers, ask the audience to discuss among themselves the one word they would choose. If you like, play some game-showy-type music for 15 seconds.

Debrief the words from the audience. You'll be able to respond with a few chuckles.

Then ask the panelists to reveal their words *at the same time*. Drum roll, please! Have the first panelist share and then ask a short probing question as to why it was answered that way. Do the same thing for all the panelists so they all have a shot at answering the question. If two panelists answered virtually identically, ask a probing, follow up question that either builds on or elicits a different response from the first one answered.

You can also take a quick poll by asking the audience for a show of hands, "Who had the same answer as panelist #1?" Then #2? Then #3? Reflect back the rough percentage of hands you see. This usually inspires a few gasps, ah-has or a laugh. One of the panelists will always pick an interesting word. For example, one panelist said "flawsome." How quirky is that? It certainly gets some talk started.

A few things to consider:

- This should be done quickly. Don't dawdle. Keep it moving. Involve the audience. You're setting the tone for the entire discussion.

- Depending on the number of panelists (best with three or four), you might want to keep it at one or two rounds initially. You can also do another round mid-way through to break up or refocus the discussion.

- These signs make a great photo opportunity. Gather the panelists together with their boards or have audience members pose with theirs. Share them on social media and attach pics to your follow-up email to the panelists and meeting organizer.

- In preparation, buy some foam board, cut into 2'x3' individual boards along with a few black, King Size Sharpie markers, enough for each panelist. Put one or two boards and a marker next to each panelist's chair. If you're going to ask two or three questions, it's a nice touch to have a different color board for each question, but be sure to use light colors. And don't forget to give the panelists a heads up that they're going to have to write a few words legibly on the board.

Make sure each of your panelists has a piece of cardstock (paper is too flimsy) and thick black marker at the ready.

Have the audience type their comments into the chatbox or into a crowdsourcing app such as Slido.com for all to see. You can even show a word cloud as it develops.

DRESS THE PART 54

Your appearance sends a signal to the audience. Dressing appropriately helps to establish your credibility and trustworthiness, but it doesn't necessarily help you engage the audience—unless you do the unexpected. You can intentionally alter your appearance so that your audience is excited and surprised and remembers your message.

Think about the topic, the theme of the conference, or the host company's slogan. Is there some way you can dress it up to add a touch of flare and excitement to the panel?

Here are a few possibilities:

DON A COSTUME. Wear something connected to your topic: a flashy tie, a feathered hat, or a jacket. Frank Kelly started a panel discussion with an example of the power of first impressions. "I wear a suit that's one size too large, have bad posture, and carry a piece of paper. I start, in a very monotonous voice, 'Um, yes. I'm here to talk to you about leaving a lasting impression.'" Just as the audience begins to fidget and feel uncomfortable, he changes his demeanor and takes off the ill-fitting suit to reveal a well-tailored one beneath.

DRESS UP. As part of the event invitation, ask the panelists to wear their favorite sports jersey, Hawaiian shirt, or a specific color. Or perhaps they can come dressed for a character in your panel. Professional speaker and Internet marketer Tom Antion tells a story about moderating a panel of senior managers of a pizza franchise. "I asked one of the panelists to march into the meeting wearing a filthy doctor's lab coat with ketchup all over it (fake blood). I had another panelist come in with a crisp, new lab coat. I asked a simple question: 'Which manager would you like operating on you?' Of course, all the junior managers yelled out that they wouldn't let either one of these people operate on them. Everyone was laughing and joking around, but the point was made. Keep employees looking clean and neat because nice customers won't want to be served by grungy food service workers."

PLAY A CHARACTER. The ultimate visual combines all these techniques together to become a character within your presentation. During a heated panel discussion with author Sasscer Hill, the moderator came dressed in a referee shirt, hat, and whistle and he moderated the panel as if he was the referee at a soccer match!

You can still dress the part – just keep in mind you'll only be visible from the waist up (unless you position your camera otherwise). Beware of wearing the same color as the background or green when using a green screen.

55 SHOW AND TELL

Remember elementary school where you brought in an item for show and tell? You can do the same thing by asking panelists to bring a prop directly related to their passion about the topic.

Simply put, props bring your words to life. You can use props to strengthen your audience's ability to visualize, understand, accept, and remember an idea, concept, or theme during the panel discussion. Many panelists may struggle with this technique, so give them a few examples to help spur their thinking:

ENHANCERS. For a panel about oyster restoration in the Chesapeake Bay, one panelist brought an actual local oyster, another brought in a replica of a non-native oyster, and another brought in a piece of aqua farming material. It set the context in real-world terms. These props enhanced our understanding and appreciation for the topic.

THEATRICAL. Actors use props to help the audience believe and follow what they are saying. Moderators and panelists can too. For example, hold up the magazine or book you are quoting. (See Case Study at the end of Chapter 10).

METAPHORICAL. Metaphorical props are used to make or reinforce your point. For example, show a Slinky® to illustrate the need for flexibility, or a telescoping spyglass to show how strategic, business, and operational plans all need to be integrated with each other.

MODEL. A model is a representation (usually smaller) of an object, person, or concept. Although you cannot bring a bulldozer into the panel discussion, you can certainly bring a toy bulldozer with you. Doctors often point to an organ model as they explain a physiological problem.

In a pinch, you can authorize one slide that is a picture of the prop—just in case they can't bring it to the panel because it's too big, too small, too dangerous, or too weird. See Tip #94—How to Use a Prop.

The audience should be able to see the entire prop within their field of vision of your camera. If they need to see detail, you need to hold it close to the camera. Or share your screen to show a picture of the prop. Or take us on a tour of your home, office, or location.

POINT/COUNTERPOINT 56

Provided you know the panelists' positions on the topic, you can frame the discussion with a quick Point/Counterpoint. Ask one panelist, "What's your main point on this topic in 15 seconds?" then ask for an alternative view on the topic in the same amount of time. Depending on the topic, you can have more than two counterpoints; offering several different points of view.

If you are relatively sure there is some diversity of opinions in the room, you can divide the room between positions: All those "for" on one side of the room and those "against" on the other side of the room. Or set up a continuum between two points from one side of the room to the other. Then ask for discussion on why they hold that position.

After a minute, debrief the room. I like to bounce from side to side, asking "Why do you support this?" A debate of sort ensues with each side quickly stating positions and rebuttals.

> Obviously, in the virtual world, you won't be able to line people up in a room. However, you can post a continuum on the screen and ask the participants to annotate where they fall on that continuum.

57 QUICKLY INTRODUCE PANELISTS

Presumably, the bios are already published (either in the program or meeting app), 99% of the attendees already know the panelists, and/or nobody really cares about the credentials anyway. (I should know; I have a string of letters behind my name. No. One. Cares.)

If you *must* introduce the panelists, here are a few tips:

KEEP IT SHORT. Just because a panelist sent their long bio, CV, or resume, doesn't mean you have to use it all. Create a two sentence bio for each panelist that quickly establishes why that person is uniquely qualified to be there.

KNOW THEIR NAMES. Not only should you know how to pronounce their names, but you should also be consistent in the application. Use all first names (Hillary). Or use the honorific (Secretary Clinton), but don't mix them up! (Hillary and Mr. Trump is just awkward.)

MAKE IT INTERESTING. You may want to include an interesting comment on a position he is taking, why she is so passionate about the topic, why he was selected to be on the panel, or just something quirky about each.

WATCH FOR BIASES. As you strive to make it interesting, there are some significant, subconscious biases that come into play—especially when the moderator extemporizes an introduction.

KEEP IT CONSISTENT. To prevent biases, make sure the introductions are equitable and have a similar length and style.

MEMORIZE IT. Another way to prevent these biases is to memorize the introductions. I know, that's more work for you, but the audience will appreciate your cheerful eye contact. If you must, read from a large index card. (For more complex panels, I use index cards as prompts for welcoming remarks, panelist introductions, key questions for each panelist and closing remarks. I also buy a circle ring at an office supply store to keep them all together and in order.)

CREATE A VISUAL. Give the audience a visual cue as to which panelist is which. The typical method is to create name tents which rest on a white draped table (ugh! Boring!). I prefer a simple slide that has the picture, name, title, a few key attributes and Twitter handle for each panelist *in the order in which they are seated*. This technique also gives the audience the sense that they are in good hands and the moderator is prepared.

BOTTOM LINE. Introductions, if you are going to do them, should be brief, informative, professional and warm with a similar length and style. Your goal is to ensure attendees are willing to listen and participate in the panel discussions.

CASE STUDY
ACES PANEL

I'm always on the lookout for creative panel discussion formats, so when I found a panel using Dr. Seuss hats, I was intrigued. I called Jane Stevens, founder of ACEs Connection and panel moderator of the session on Trauma-informed and Resilience-building Communities: The Journey of ACEs Heroes at the Adverse Childhood Experiences conference.

Here's the backstory: Her panel was sandwiched between two high-powered "make 'em laugh, make 'em cry" speakers on the deadly afternoon of the last day of the conference. So she was challenged to make this panel extraordinary.

The premise of the panel was based on a video animation by Matthew Winkler. He, in turn, was inspired by Joseph Campbell, who explored the common themes of a hero's journey from stories around the world in his book, *The Hero with a Thousand Faces.* The objective of the panel was to describe the hero's journey and to let others know what to expect and that they are not alone.

So Stevens wrote a rap song and then shared it with her panelists. Initially, they were shocked (whaattt? This isn't going to be your typical panel discussion?), but once they realized what she was trying to do, they got into it too. Then one of the panelists quipped that it sounded more like Dr. Seuss than rap and they all agreed. One of the panelists offered to buy some Dr. Seuss hats. Another offered to buy some large storybooks and recover them in the panel theme and put the ACEs story in the books so they could read it onstage and a creative format was born!

Here's what they did:
- Sauntered on stage with upbeat music: Sly and the Family Stone's "Everyday People". (Yeah, yeah!)
- Moderator Stevens introduced the topic on building communities and the hero's journey. She then introduced the panelists.
- Then, "like magicians, the four people on stage pulled out Dr. Seuss hats—all, broad brimmed hats with the familiar red and white stripes—and put them on their heads. They all opened up what looked like children's books, and taking turns, each started to take the audience along for an ACEs journey. The surprise was that the story—scripted by Stevens—about a girl named Patience, was all in Seuss-like rhyme." [How clever!] As they were telling the story, a slideshow was running with Stevens advancing the slides at specific points in the story.
- Then each of the panelists shared their own journeys of integrating practices based on ACEs science in their communities. The panelists started with a chapter title and described their experiences much like a story to be told to the audience.
- To summarize the presentations, Stevens showed the "Mapping the Movement" map, a network of networks that features many health initiatives across the globe.
- The panel concluded with a short poem—a call to action for the audience:

Now that we've come to the grand finale,
Here's the moral of this remarkable story.
You all are heroes or soon can be.
Now that you know ACEs science, you can rally.
You're called to adventure
You're accepting the challenge
You're conquering your fear
And saying: I can manage!
To change the world.
All you have to do...
...says Teri Barila...
Is rock around this clock
And then start over.

And, because they had a bit more time, they invited everyone in the audience to introduce themselves to another person and share their own hero's story.

Doesn't this sound like an entertaining, creative panel?

Stevens said it was very well received and people continued to discuss their own hero's journeys even after the session was over. That's what panel discussions are all about.

As I was finishing my call with Stevens, she said, "This experience has encouraged me to think more creatively about panels from now on." I hope this case study and book encourages you to do that as well.

CHAPTER SEVEN
INSPIRE A LIVELY AND INFORMATIVE CONVERSATION

The moderator needs to embrace the role of interlocutor. When panelists say something interesting, or confusing, you should jump in with a follow-up. "Tell me more," you could say, or "What do you mean by that?" or "Can you explain that in more detail?" That enables the conversation to go deeper, away from the panelists' typical talking points and into more fruitful territory.

~ Dorie Clark

THE CONVERSATION WILL START TO FLOW on its own *if* you have prepared the panelists appropriately, and you kick off the discussion with a few good questions. Encourage each panelist to comment on particular parts of other panelists' statements.

Be flexible about following the natural conversation path, as long as it is interesting and the audience is engaged. You may, however, need to interject a follow-up question here and there to keep things moving at a brisk pace. An energy lull can be devastating.

This chapter provides you with several techniques to keep the conversation moving and feeling lively.

HOW TO INSPIRE CONVERSATION

A key skill of any panel moderator is to inspire conversation between panelists. After the initial remarks (such as an initial presentation or an initial hot potato question), listen for areas of agreement *or* disagreement to inspire conversation. Whether the panelists are in agreement or not, summarize common theme(s) and decide on a path forward:

STEP 1   **ASK OPEN-ENDED QUESTIONS** to get more information.
Draw them out in a way that doesn't imply either a correct answer or assume responsibility:

- "What are your thoughts on...?"
- "How might we do this?"
- "What are your ideas about...?"
- "Would you please say some more about...?"
- "Can you help us to understand your perspective?"
- "How do you see that working?"

STEP 2   **BUILD ON WHAT HAS BEEN SAID** to deepen or extend the thinking:

- Connect/summarize the comments and then pose a question.
- "You mentioned...Could you say more about that?"

STEP 3   **ASK FOR CLARIFICATION** to gain a clearer understanding of what has been said:

- "What do you mean by...?"
- "When you say...How do you see that working?"

STEP 4   **CHECK FOR UNDERSTANDING** to confirm key points.
Paraphrase, rephrase, or ask for agreement or correction:

- "What I hear you saying is..."
- "As I understand it..."
- "Let me see if I understand what you are saying..."
- "So you think (hope, feel, believe)..."

STEP 5   **SEGUE** to transition the conversation.
If you don't like the tone of the conversation, or the direction it's taking, shift the conversation by asking a new question.

ANYTIME   **LET IT GO!**
Use a little humor to diffuse any tension and shift focus to another area. No need to dig at something that is distracting, just move along.

The challenge for any moderator is to choose the right path forward to instill an interesting and lively conversation.

ASK FOLLOW-UP QUESTIONS 58

As a panel moderator, there is a distinct art to asking follow-up questions during a discussion. These are questions you ask to probe further into a specific aspect of the conversation. The key is to listen intently to what each panelist is saying, and where appropriate, decide how to dig deeper into the topic:

ADVANCE THE CONVERSATION

- *Play Back a Key Word or Phrase.* If a panelist says, "I found the results to be quite disturbing" you can follow up by asking, "What was so disturbing?"

- *Build on What Has Been Said.* In order to deepen or extend the thinking, add to what was said, such as "You mentioned X. Could you tell us more about that? How did you accomplish so much in such little time?"

- *Probe for More Information.* When a nugget is left dangling, dig a little deeper to extract more specific information.

ADVANCE THE PLOT

- *Go On…* When a panelist tells part of a story, encourage them to continue. For example, if a panelist shares a story about the struggle they faced in executing their strategy, you could ask them to continue: "Once you started to see some traction, what happened next?"

- *Reflect It.* Let's say one panelist has a strong opinion. Ask another panelist if they share that same opinion. If not, then ask them to share the differing viewpoint.

- *Share Information.* If you, as a moderator, have some information to advance the conversation, share it quickly and concisely combined with a specific question directed to one of the panelists.

- *Dig Deeper.* When a panelist makes a claim that just doesn't sound quite right, question it on behalf of the audience. Ask for an example, metrics, or sources to substantiate the claim.

- *Stir the Pot.* Look for areas of disagreement between panelists. Ask a panelist for a contradictory point of view. "Brian just stated X. Alice, what is your view on X?"

- *Ask for the Devil.* If the panel is in complete agreement, don't just stir the pot because you can. Although, if you know there is something deeper to explore, ask a panelist or an audience member to serve as a devil's advocate and argue the other side of the issue.

FOCUS THE CONVERSATION

- *Clarify a Point.* When a panelist is too vague, ask for further information to clarify or expand the point. Clarifying questions typically start with a who, what, when, where, or a why.

- *Catch Contradictions.* You have to be on your toes to catch panelists contradicting themselves. "Charlie, you just mentioned X, and earlier you mentioned Y. They seem at odds with each other. Please clarify your position."

- *Pull Out of the Weeds.* If a panelist is being too specific, ask them to share the larger significance of their point or how it connects to the big picture.

- *Pull Out of the Clouds.* If a panelist is being too abstract, push for specifics. Ask for examples, case studies. or anecdotes that illustrate the larger point.

- *Check for Understanding.* Perhaps the panelist is a bit obtuse and you're not sure the audience understands the point. Paraphrase the panelist's comment and ask, "Let me see if I've got this right."

SYNTHESIZE THE CONVERSATION

- *Make Bridges.* Look for opportunities to connect two ideas together. "Andy, that's an interesting point you just made about A. Cathy, earlier you referenced B. Are these ideas related? Do you need one to accomplish the other?"

- *Connect the Dots.* Take pieces of information shared by the panelists and then pose a question that infers a logical consequence of the previous comments. "Sally, you mentioned X, and Rashid said Y, does that mean we have Z?" or "Does that still hold true?"

- *Test the Unsaid.* Sometimes, the real issue has not been spoken. If you sense there is something which hasn't been said, test it out. "If we do this, are you concerned about...?" Or "I'm wondering if you might be concerned about...?"

- *Test for Agreement.* Check for the apparent agreement (or disagreement) with others by asking, "How do you feel about what Mike said?" or "How many of you agree with this?"

AIM FOR APPLICATION

- *5 Ws and an H.* Aim for application to the real world versus a lot of theory. Explore the issues with impromptu and relevant questions that start with Who, What, Where, When, Why and How.

SEGUE

- *Shift Gears.* When you have covered one topic enough, don't be afraid to shift the focus forward. (See Chapter 10)

- *Create Transitions.* Before you move from one topic to another, summarize the key points and bring it back to the core topic. These transitions should mark key threads in the conversation.

- *Heads Up.* Two minutes before the end of a section, let the audience know that you will be moving into the next section (usually audience Q&A), the process you will be using (line up at the microphone, raise hands, use SMS, tweet) and the ground rules. This gives them time to think about their questions so you can launch right into the Q&A session.

QUESTION BEHIND THE QUESTION 59

Try the question behind the question; a technique where a *panelist* can probe deeper into the topic.

The moderator asks an interesting question to all of the panelists (or a specific panelist) and the panelist answers, "Actually, let's answer the question behind that question." The panelist then shares what the real issue is, thus, showing their brilliance on the topic.

Let's listen in on a real-life example from a panel at the National Speakers Association where Extreme Meetings Moderator Brian Walter modeled this technique he created:

MODERATOR: Let's start with David. When should a speaker realize they should be spending a lot more money on their marketing?

DAVID: Let's ask the question behind the question. Why is that speaker not getting enough bookings?

SYLVIE: From the marketing, they already have.

DAVID: So, why is the speaker not getting enough bookings from the marketing that they already have in place?

MODERATOR: Ahhhh. Now that is a deeper question!

You'll need to coach your panelists to ask the question behind the question where appropriate. Or you can nudge the conversation along by pointedly asking the panelists, "So what's the question behind that question?" It always generates interesting conversation during a panel discussion.

Depending upon your topic, your panelists, and their comfort level with showing their expertise, you can use this technique two or three times. You wouldn't want to do it more often than that.

60 SHARE AN EXAMPLE OR ILLUSTRATION

Tell an interesting story. An easy way to spark some interest in your panel discussion is to start with an example or an illustration. By doing so, your panelists can provide depth, substance, and nuance to the topic, setting the tone for an intriguing panel discussion.

You may be wondering: what's the difference between an example and an illustration?

EXAMPLES are short statements to clarify or elaborate on a point, usually expressed in one or two sentences. They are often prefaced with "for example" or "for instance." When sharing an example, try to refer to specific people in the audience as a whole to demonstrate or make your point. An example of this would be "You can easily engage your audience during a panel discussion using myriad techniques. For example, you can periodically poll the audience, ask for questions from the audience, or ask a question to discuss in a small group."

ILLUSTRATIONS. When you're looking to extend an example, use an illustration to provide more detail in order to clarify your point. The best illustrations use specific names, dates, and locations, as appropriate. Generally, an illustration describes a process or chronology of events and provides a level of concreteness that is easily remembered. "The moderator really engages the audience during a panel discussion. How? Let me give you an illustration. At the panel discussion last week, the moderator crowdsourced audience questions using the meeting app."

It never fails.

Providing a bit more depth and detail is a sure-fire way to spark a little interest in your panel discussion.

SPILL SECRETS 61

Everyone likes a good story, especially when it's a train wreck! So how do you get your panelists to spill the goods?

Brian Walter, founder of Extreme Meetings recommends that you ask your question in such a way that compels them to answer in the form of a story or an anecdote.

For example, you can ask a question like:

- Tell us about a time when...
- Have you ever...?

When you ask a story question correctly, the panelist can't do anything BUT tell a story about the time when...

What's even better is that because the panelist shared a real-world story, there's a bit of vulnerability creeping onto the stage. And with that vulnerability, the audience sees the panelist as a human, sees themselves reflected in the story, and likes the panel even more.

HOW TO ASK A STORY-QUESTION

STEP 1   **FRAME THE PROBLEM**
Frame a problem that the majority of the audience members are experiencing. This could be a recurring problem, challenge or fear.

STEP 2   **ASK A QUESTION**
Reframe that problem into a question that requires a story for the panelist to answer:

- "Tell us about a time when you..."
- "Give us an example when you..."
- "When did you find yourself in a position where you had to...?"

STEP 3   **SELECT A PANELIST TO ANSWER**
Look at the facial reactions of the panelists. Are they smiling or nodding? Are they looking away? Are they looking directly at you and not in a good way? It's your judgment on who to ask.

After the panelist spills, you can decide if this is a one-and-done question. You have several options:

1. You could keep going. It could be that the answer was awesome and requires a follow-up question—a question that you know the audience is dying to ask.
2. You could emphasize the lesson learned from this experience.
3. You could ask the same question to another willing panelist.
4. You could ask a different awesome story question.

By asking a question that requires a story, you put them in a position of being vulnerable, charming, or self-deprecating. The audience will lean in and remember that story and the point long after the panel discussion.

62 AVOID THE HOT POTATO & PING PONG

I recently attended a panel discussion at a large conference where the moderator started the session with a hot potato and shifted to ping pong. The result? No real conversation ensued because the moderator was too controlling. He never gave permission to the panelists to engage in a meaningful conversation. Instead, everything had to be funneled through him.

So, you may ask, what is the Hot Potato and the Ping Pong? Here are my definitions:

The **HOT POTATO** is when a moderator asks the same question to each of the panelists until each panelist has weighed in. I always feel sorry for panelist Z who is usually robbed of anything new to say or time has run out and they have to rush.

The **PING PONG** is when the moderator asks a different question to each of the panelists, but it always comes back to the moderator to ask more questions.

Both of these techniques are useful—until they become the *only* questioning techniques the moderator has in the tool bag.

For example, The Ping Pong is an effective technique to start the conversation. You have to start somewhere, so have a unique, separate question for each panelist, tailored to highlight some specific aspect of that panelist's background. Just make sure you have the same level question (softie or hardball, but not both) for everyone else on the panel. You don't want to seem unfair by giving a softie question to your favorite panelist and then going in for the kill with a hardball question to a different panelist.

The Hot Potato is a good technique to close the session and get a sound bite or summary idea from each panelist. For example, "In 30 seconds or less, what's the one thing you think our audience should do as a result of being at this panel session today?"

Although both of these techniques have their strengths, Ping Pong and Hot Potato are not effective as the only questioning techniques a moderator should use. Both of these techniques keep the focal point on the moderator when it should be on the conversation between the panelists. Use them sparingly and purposefully and you'll be fine.

KEEP THE CONVERSATION MOVING 63

A panel moderator's most important responsibility is to keep the conversation flowing naturally. Like a good talk show host, here are 11 tips to keep the keep the conversation lively and informative:

1. **USE YOUR QUESTIONS.** Get the panelists to talk by using your well-prepared conversation starter questions. Make it sound like you just thought of them and make sure each question is directed to a specific panelist.

2. **BREAK EYE CONTACT.** Look at the panelist when asking a question, then turn to the audience to gauge their reaction and interest. If you look at the panelists after you've asked a question, the panelist will instinctively look back at you when responding. You really want the panelists to talk among themselves and with the audience.

3. **WATCH FOR CUES.** In your pre-meeting, you should set up a way for panelists to catch your eye to let you and the other panelists know that they would like to respond. Your panelists should be able to tell you and each other with a glance that they want to address a question or follow up on someone else's comments.

4. **TWO IS ENOUGH.** Don't ask every panelist every question. By the time the fifth panelist is answering the same question four other panelists have answered, the contribution is probably pretty thin. When you ask a question, two answers are plenty, unless a third person is dying to jump in.

5. **BE FLEXIBLE.** Be open and flexible about following the natural conversation path as long as it is interesting and the audience is engaged. Be willing to let go of your planned questions should a particularly interesting line of discussion emerge.

6. **TAKE NOTES.** Especially when the panelists deliver prepared remarks, listen very carefully and capture important statements verbatim so you can refer to them during the discussion.

7. **BE NEUTRAL.** Never say "I agree with..." Your role is to be neutral and facilitate the conversation, not to weigh in or offer your opinion.

8. **INVITE COMMENTS.** Encourage panelists to comment on particular parts of other panelists' statements. Stay away from a general, "What do you think about that?" It opens the door to off-topic answers.

9. **USE HUMOR.** Use humor gently and appropriately in service of the discussion. Use your natural wit to lighten the moment. Beware of going too far with canned jokes, gimmicks, and sarcasm. It's a panel, not a game show.

10. **BANTER.** Encourage the panelists to have fun, chatter, and joke among themselves.

11. **BE QUIET.** You don't need to interject a question, comment or make a witty observation after each panelist speaks. Let the conversation flow until it isn't flowing well.

Follow these 11 tips and you'll have a great conversation during your panel discussion.

64 BALANCE AIRTIME

One of the core values for all moderators is the notion of fairness. Every panelist should have roughly the same number of questions to answer, the same type of questions (hardball to softie), and the same amount of time to speak. When that doesn't happen, it becomes glaringly obvious.

There are five ways a panelist gets airtime and *all* of them are in the hands of the moderator:

1. The moderator asks a direct question to a panelist.
2. The moderator allows a panelist to respond because the panelist's name was invoked in a question or in a response (known as a rebuttal).
3. The moderator selects a panelist to respond to another panelist's remarks.
4. The moderator fails to intervene and allows a panelist to speak beyond the time limits set at the beginning of the panel or what is appropriate for the session.
5. The panelist so strongly butts into the conversation that the moderator yields the floor to that panelist.

Pay attention to who is contributing and how long, then take active steps to balance it out:

- Ask quieter panelists whether they have anything to add before you move on to another question.
- Address new questions first to people who have spoken less.
- Look for the quieter panelists who are trying to interject and facilitate their interruption.
- Tell a panelist to keep their answer brief (or to hold it entirely) for the sake of time.
- Restate or reframe the question and direct it to a quieter panelist.
- Interrupt a panelist if they're taking an unacceptable amount of time.
- When many panelists want to speak, create a queue where you identify those who haven't spoken as much first, then who will speak next, and next.

Stephanie Zvan says, "I know it can feel rude to signal to a speaker that they're talking too much, but it's also rude to your other panelists and to your audience to let one or two people dominate the discussion. People committed their time to your event expecting a panel, not a speech."

> Keep a list of who speaks, how often and how long.
> Notice the gaps and target who should get the next question.

PRACTICE 65

Let's take a poll. How many of you practice moderating your panel like you would for a speech? Most savvy presenters map out a speech, write the dialogue, and practice several times, all while editing their notes. Finally, they rehearse the speech the whole way through so there is no need for notes, cue cards or teleprompter.

Do panel moderators do that too?

My anecdotal answer is no, not really. Not to the extent of a full-blown speech.

Why is that? The event itself is just as important. You're asking participants to invest their valuable time. Nowadays, there is a substantial probability that someone is taking a video and/or tweeting about the event—saving the good, bad, and the ugly for posterity.

Once you've done all the planning, take the time to legitimately practice the flow of the panel discussion. Some parts should be memorized (your introduction of the topic and the panelists as well as the closing). Others you need to vocalize (the sequence of questions) so you are completely comfortable with them and can easily shift them around. And when you switch gears, practice the transitions from one segment to another.

The point of all this practicing is so that you, as the panel moderator, can be completely present to the conversation in the moment—making sure that the audience is getting great value from the panelists. As a result, you'll look brilliant.

66 REINFORCE THE DRUMBEAT

I'm often asked how you get panelists, who are used to being extremely polite, to be more conversational. Especially if they've served on many otherwise boring panels. This can be a real challenge.

I suggest a conversational drumbeat so that each and every time you reach out to your panelists, you keep telling them that this is a conversation.

DRUMBEAT 1. It all starts with the invitation and setting expectations. Whether you are inviting them to participate by phone or by email, let your panelists know that this panel will be *conversational*. Perhaps the format will be a bit different. Or the fact that you are engaging the audience early on in the discussion. Confirm that this is a panel *discussion*; not a presentation.

DRUMBEAT 2. During your prep call, emphasize the importance of making the panel a conversation. If you can, have the conference organizers on the call or at the meet up reinforcing that message as well.

DRUMBEAT 3. During the meet up the day of the panel, reinforce the conversational intention. Panel moderator Kate Delaney pumps them up by saying, "We just want to have a conversation here. You are the barracudas. You have this incredible information. It's amazing we have you here! I just want to get as much out to this audience as we can in a conversational way."

DRUMBEAT 4. Right before the session starts, remind them: "This is a conversation. Don't worry. Just let it flow. Follow your instincts. Just have a conversation like we're all sitting around discussing something really valuable and important to the people who are listening. Don't be afraid to jump in. You have a point to make, or somebody says something and you don't agree, or you want to add to it, just go for it."

DRUMBEAT 5. As you are introducing the topic and the format to the audience, re-emphasize the goal of the panel is to have a completely unscripted, spontaneous conversation for the benefit of the audience.

When the panelists hear this drumbeat repeated, they are likely to understand that you're looking for a conversational panel discussion.

MANAGE TIME EFFECTIVELY 67

Your audience can get really annoyed when the moderator doesn't manage time well during a panel discussion. All it takes is for the moderator to take a smidge more time with opening remarks, the panelists introductions, or presentations to go on a little longer, or the panelists to take forever to answer a question. Soon the panel runs out of time to get to the audience's questions. You want to avoid this.

Try these 10 tips to manage time effectively during a panel discussion:

1. **START ON TIME AND END ON TIME.** Seems simple to say, but not so easy. Make every effort to start on time and always end on time, especially if there are subsequent sessions on the program. Try keeping a clock visible so everyone can see the time.

2. **CREATE A DETAILED WORKING AGENDA.** Create an agenda that includes timeframes around the opening remarks, introductions, presentations, moderator-curated questions, audience Q&A and closing remarks. Be realistic in your expectations and write them down.

3. **ALERT PANELISTS.** During the preparation phase, let the panelists know the format, agenda and ground rules. Encourage them to be concise in their comments and to limit their comments to no more than one or two minutes. They probably won't remember what you've said, so follow up with an email to confirm the details.

4. **REMIND THE PANELISTS.** Right before the panel starts, remind them of the timeframes and ground rules. As you meet up with the panelists, these quick reminders are great prevention strategies. You can even hand them a reminder card with the agenda and timeframes.

5. **REVIEW THE AGENDA.** During the beginning of the panel, review the agenda, the process and ground rules again. When everybody knows the game plan, people stay focused and on track.

6. **FOLLOW YOUR AGENDA.** You have a well-thought out process in place. Trust the process and follow the agenda.

7. **REVIEW TIME LIMITS.** If time is going to be an issue, set some time limits before a panelist answers a question—especially with those who can tend to babble on.

8. **CONGRATULATE.** When a panelist keeps to the time limit when answering a question, affirm the good behavior by saying, "Thank you for that concise answer."

9. **INTERVENE FIRMLY AND GRACEFULLY.** When a panelist or audience member goes off topic, takes too much time, or is content clueless, you need to step in on behalf of the audience. (Check out Tip #68—The Top 10 Times to Intervene.)

10. **ACKNOWLEDGE WHEN RUNNING BEHIND.** When you are running behind schedule, let the panelists and audience know what's going on. When everyone knows you're cognizant and watching the clock, they'll breathe easier and let you take responsibility for catching up and ending on time or at a new negotiated end time.

CASE STUDY
SPILL SECRETS

Since I routinely troll the internet for examples of panel discussions, my Google alert sent me an email for the panel: *Crowdfunding Experts Spill Their Secrets For a Successful Campaign.*

That title got my attention.

Panelists spilled their secrets; sharing something new; something the audience hadn't heard before.

I've referred to this as the Wizard of Oz moment where audiences want to get a peek behind the curtain. See how it's really done. Get the insider scoop.

What was particularly intriguing about this panel was that the panel moderator asked the panelists to lay out a "strategic timeline for the most critical period of any [crowdfunding] campaign hoping to gain traction." As they discussed the roadmap, the moderator, Ryan Foland, who is known for his speaking and stick figure drawing skills, pulled out his iPad to draw a roadmap for all to see. In essence, they were co-creating a crowdfunding path for the audience to use *beyond* the panel discussion.

After the panel, he shared the drawing on Twitter.

Now that's a Wizard of Oz moment!

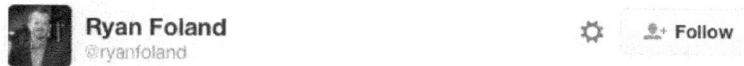

Ryan Foland
@ryanfoland   ⚙ 👤+ Follow

Awesome #crowdfunding panel at #DigitalHollywood with @Expert_Dojo, @JasonGoyer and @justingiddings. See attached road map we came up with!

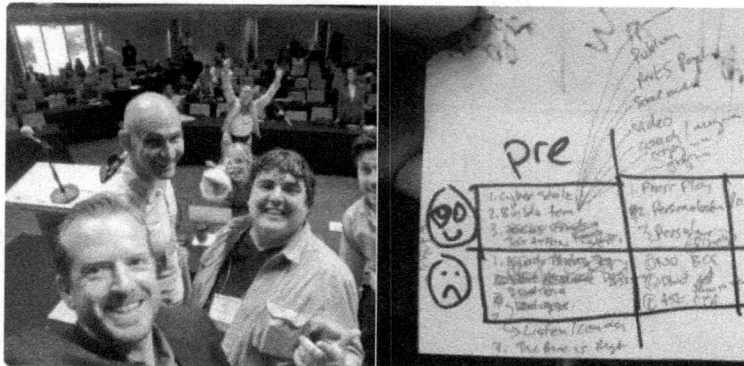

CHAPTER EIGHT
INTERVENE FIRMLY BUT TACTFULLY

Making panelists look smart does not mean letting them bull shitake the audience. My theory is that the moderator is called the moderator because her role is to ensure that there is only a moderate level of bull shitake and sales pitches. A good moderator is the audience's advocate for truth, insight, and brevity—any two will do. When a panelist makes a sales pitch or tells lies, you are morally obligated to smack him around in front of the audience.

~ Guy Kawasaki

AS THE MODERATOR, you are the audience's chief advocate. If someone's boring you, then they are boring the audience for sure. If you think they're going on too long and not making their point, you need to intervene.

The good news about your panel of experts is that they know A LOT about their issue and are used to talking extensively about it. You need to make sure they understand the ground rules and when and how you will intervene.

The best way to intervene is to *prevent* the problem from happening in the first place.

Then, when a panelist or audience member steps over the line, you can point to a prevention strategy or ground rule you've put into place:

- Reinforce the topic, purpose, and guidelines at the beginning.
- Alert panelists to the fact that all time limits will be strictly observed.
- Create a signal for them as they come to the end of their time limit.

68   WHEN YOU MUST INTERVENE

Regardless of how prestigious your panelists are, as well as the intense preparation you put into your session, you must intervene at times. The most frequent situations are when a panelist commits any of these actions that have the potential to destroy your discussion.

FILIBUSTERS. For the long-winded panelists that go on with no conclusion in sight. It's good information, but they are just taking way too long to express their idea. You should have a pre-negotiated signal between you and the panelists, so hopefully, they'll take a cue from you. If not, when they take a breath, politely intervene. Cut in and shift the focus to another panelist. Start with that pre-negotiated cue.

HAS DIARRHEA OF THE MOUTH. Unlike the filibusterer, you might run into a panelist who babbles, rambles, and goes on and on and on. Unfortunately, you have no idea what the panelist just said. If you can't follow the conversation and can't pinpoint a message, ask, "Excuse me, that was a lot of information. Can you please headline that into one sentence?" Mark Diamond also suggests tightening up the conversation by "injecting key questions at the right time: 'I hear what you are saying, but how do you really make this work in your legal department?' [or] drawing out interesting content."

DOMINATES. Although you have encouraged your panelists not to dominate, a panel hog seems to always answer the questions first and have something to say, regardless if another panelist has already made the point. Watch for when they breathe and interject in a nice way. Comment on their opinion and ask a complementary question to a panelist who hasn't had the opportunity to contribute as much. If this behavior continues, start calling on specific panelists to answer the questions. Unfortunately, that cuts down the lively banter and exchange between the panelists, but that's better than giving in to the dominator.

VEERS OFF TOPIC. Although you do all the right things to set up the panel at the beginning, the conversation may veer off topic. Although this new conversation may be very stimulating, you owe it to the audience to make sure the content matches the promotional material. Scott Stratten says, "People pick which concurrent session to go to based on that write up, which means they aren't going to another...If you don't deliver on your promise, not only is there a letdown, but a missed opportunity to see another session that may have been more suitable." On the other hand, sometimes you NEED to veer off topic. It's a strategic moment. Check in with the audience and if they clearly want to go off in this new direction, be flexible and adapt.

INTERRUPTS OTHERS. It's downright annoying when one panelist constantly interrupts another. After this happens a few times, make sure the current panelist finishes their contribution before you designate or allow another panelist to react. You might intervene with, "Let's let Safra finish her thought."

IS HOSTILE. It doesn't happen often, but sometimes you'll get a hostile panelist who blatantly doesn't want to be there—and will let everyone know. Or, a panelist displays dismay by not answering questions. Hopefully, you have scoped this out in your planning, but you may run into this rather awkward and uncomfortable situation. You can either ignore it (which if the panelist is ignoring you, it's not a problem until AFTER the panel when accusations will fly), or you can call a spade a spade. "I see that you're upset about this. What about this topic is so disconcerting?"

IS CONTENT CLUELESS. Panelists may mention something that's startling, confusing, or controversial and then they'll just continue on as if it's common knowledge or they don't want to explain anymore. "Don't let this happen," cautions David Spark, founder of Spark Media Solutions. "It leaves a huge gap in the discussion. If the question popped into your head, it's probably popped into the head of everyone in the room. Don't always rely on your own judgment. As a moderator, you might not fit into the audience demographic. What you know, and what the audience knows, can be drastically different." Don't be afraid to ask the question everyone in the room wants to ask.

PITCHES A PRODUCT. Your audience has spent time and money to attend this panel discussion; they don't want to hear sales pitches from the panelists. When one vendor talks about how great his company or product is, then the next panelist will feel compelled to do the same and before you know it, you have an hour long commercial. Hopefully you've had a prevention strategy to alert your panelists that you'll intervene promptly. Then do so if they dare to transgress.

TOO POLITE. Scott Berkun says that, "For a panel to work, the panelists must be comfortable disagreeing with, or passionately supporting, each other in front of a crowd. Few professionals are willing to do this, especially if they just met the other panelists five minutes ago. They know that to openly criticize someone else is likely to make them seem like a jerk. Why take that risk?" Fair enough, Scott. In the prep work, encourage panelists to voice their opinions. Audiences LOVE a little drama, contention, and dialogue, so set the panel up to deliver something they can't get elsewhere.

EMBARRASSES ANOTHER. It happens. I wish it didn't, but you need to be prepared when one panelist humiliates another or says something snarky. You have to quickly shift the focus. Sonia Herrero says, "If anyone puts a panelist on the spot, take the spotlight yourself or maneuver it onto someone else who won't mind being center-stage for a while."

So there you have it.

The top ten naughty things panelists could do during a panel discussion and how the moderator can still make lemonade out of lemons.

> All of these escalating interventions are at your disposal in the virtual environment except movement, (although you can move your face closer to the webcam to indicate that you are watching something closely). You also have the ability to mute or cancel video from any or all participants. As a last resort, you can remove a participant from the room.

69 USE ESCALATING INTERVENTIONS

What if something else goes wrong during your panel discussion? Something you haven't thought of or prepared for? Something completely unexpected? When things go south, I suggest you use a process I call escalating interventions. You'll want to be firm, polite and fair because you often don't have a whole lot of time and want to keep the conversation moving briskly. So start with the lowest level intervention appropriate to the situation. If that doesn't modify the disruptive behavior, then kick it up a notch to the next level.

DO NOTHING. You always have the option to do nothing and see if the situation resolves itself. However, if you let one person run over, you penalize everyone else.

EYE CONTACT.

- Shoot 'em a glance when time is almost up or they're making inappropriate or irrelevant comments.
- Confidently check your watch.
- Use your pre-discussed cue.

MOVEMENT. Put a hand up, show a cue card, tap your pencil, ring a bell, move toward them, behind them, or put a hand on their shoulder.

REDIRECT THE CONVERSATION.

- Change up the questions.
- Reframe the question and direct it to another panelist.
- Rephrase the statement into something more relevant.
- Condense a panelist's answer when it's too lengthy.
- Call on someone in the audience who you know has similar issues and ask if what was just said resonates with them.
- Gently interrupt and assure them that you can discuss it later in the session if there is enough time.
- Interject at the end of a sentence or while the panelist is taking a breath.
- Ask for one conversation at a time when panelists are talking over each other.
- Transition to the next topic when the topic has been covered enough.

REMIND THEM.

- Refocus on the topic.
- Reinforce the process ground rules.
- Restate the time allocated for the comment.
- Reinforce a key point.
- Announce the time remaining for this section of the panel.

CONFRONT THE DISRUPTER. This is the highest level intervention, and you should only have to resort to this level if you have a jerk on your panel.

- Appeal to the disrupter.
- Cut off the panelist.
- Disengage.

In my experience, you will rarely climb to a confrontation, as long as you place prevention strategies in place and escalate your interventions appropriately during a panel discussion.

PREPARE CUT-OFF PHRASES 70

It's not a matter of *if* a panelist on your panel discussion will dominate the discussion, pitch a product, or ramble off-topic, it's *when* it will happen.

So why not be prepared for the inevitable?

Prepare some cut-off phrases to bring the errant panelist back on track:

- "You have an interesting point there, but we want to know more about _____."
- "Wow, that's one side of the coin. [A different panelist who hasn't had the opportunity to contribute as much], what do you think about this issue?"
- "We're going to shift gears here...[and then change the focus of the discussion]".

If someone is dominating the discussion, executive speech coach Angela DeFinis recommends that you "watch the person's natural breathing rhythm and then interject between breaths, 'Thank you, Indra. Now let's hear Jayden's perspective on this topic.'"

Then again, you can uber-prepare by asking the panelists what cutoff phrases they respond to. Tell them you will use this tactic for keeping the panel discussion focused and on time.

71 HANDLE THE VERBOSE EXPERT

When moderating a panel with a wide range of speakers (for example one bona fide expert who has written a ton of books on the subject, along with a practitioner, as well as student), the so-called-expert might dominate the discussion.

From a prevention perspective, appeal to the expert in a pre-panel chat either over the phone or F2F prior to the panel (NOT by email).

Appeal to their ego by saying something like: "I know you're the expert in the field. I've read all your books and follow your thought leadership—and I know you have a tremendous wealth of knowledge you could share during this upcoming panel discussion. In fact, you could probably just do a break-out session on your own. However, we're doing a panel discussion and it's important that you be able to present your ideas succinctly while making sure the other panelists have an equal amount of time to present their ideas."

Take it a step farther and enlist the expert's help by asking, "Would you be so kind as to help me out and make sure we are able to hear equally from all the panelists?"

A little self-awareness goes a long way, and I find that when you stroke the ego a bit and then ask for help, the expert panelist usually complies.

But then again, it may not work. So have a few techniques in your back pocket ready:

- "Kendric, that's an interesting point; Ursula, would you like to comment?"
- "Ladies first. Ursula, how about you start."
- Reframe the question and direct it to another panelist.
- Gently interrupt when the expert goes on too long. Assure the panelist that you can return to discussing that topic later on in the panel if there is enough time.
- Interject at the end of a sentence or while the panelist is taking a breath and redirect the conversation.

These intervention techniques are largely dependent on your own personal style, the topic, the ground rules you've established, the atmosphere in the room and the audience's personality.

So think through any preventions you might put into place as well as some possible interventions—and then you'll be ready.

RESIST OFFERING YOUR OPINION 72

Sad, but true. The audience is there to see you moderate, not be a panelist. If you offer your own opinions, you look like you're trying to hog time from the panelists. Do this only if your panel consists entirely of unbelievable bores, and you can bring down the house with your impromptu comedy routines. And certainly, never offer your opinion or tell a panelist they're stupid. Let another panelist say it instead.

~ Steven Robbins

Moderators who have deep expertise and opinions on the topic tend to jump into the discussion—and then who facilitates the moderator?

For some specific formats, the moderator *may* be expected to participate as well. It's not easy to combine the role of moderator and expert because that person may end up dominating the discussion and takeover the show.

There are times, however, where it *may* be appropriate for you, as the moderator, to add your own opinion and perspective to the conversation.

Here are three times where your expertise *may* be appropriate to share:

1. Opening remarks on the topic (in a balanced way) before formally posing the issue to the panelists.
2. Transitions between the last question and the next one.
3. When the question has not been adequately answered. If you have given the panelists (or the audience) the opportunity to answer and you get nothing or you have something *significant* to add, make your contribution at the end of the conversation.

A moderator's role is to make everyone else look smart while providing tremendous value to the audience. When it comes to contributing content, the moderator is the fallback just in case the wisdom isn't in the room.

Obviously, everyone has an opinion. If you have a lot to say about a topic, then you should be a *panelist* and not the moderator.

CASE STUDY
THE RANDOM RANT

It was December 2016 in Toronto, right before Donald Trump was to assume the presidency of the United States. I was moderating a panel discussion with three **D.E.E.P.** (**D**iverse, have **E**xpertise, be **E**loquent and **P**repared) panelists talking about how to scale their businesses during an industry event. The conversation was scintillating and going swimmingly well when one of the American panelists took a left turn and started ranting about Donald Trump and how horrible he will be as president.

You could see the audience literally squirming in their seats. The panelists' eyeballs started moving from side to side. It was, in a word, awkward.

Since I'm married to a Canadian, I know Canadians, by and large, are very politically aware of what's going on in the U.S. (probably more than many U.S. citizens), and are exceedingly polite. This rant was completely inappropriate and obviously a conversational path no one wanted to walk. I had do something. Quickly.

I simply cut her off mid-sentence and asked, "So what does this have to do with our topic?"

She stammered and said, "Everything," and then focused her comments on how the election might shape her business.

You could hear the collective sigh of relief from the audience.

CHAPTER NINE
FINISH WITH PANACHE

After an on stage discussion, it is really important to recap the key messages that were shared during the panel and what the big takeaways should be for audience members. This is ideally done at the end of your panel, but can also be done through some sort of recap after the event itself (I love to do blog posts as recaps of events.)

~ Rohit Bhargava

MY GOODNESS! Time is flying so fast! You've been facilitating a brilliant panel discussion, and you have just a few minutes to conclude the session.

Let the audience know that the program is coming to an end by saying, "We're almost out of time. Just a few key things to wrap up."

What are those few things?

- Summarize the key messages and takeaways.
- Housekeeping reminders.
- Thank yous to the panelists, audience and others involved.
- Next steps and directions to the next event.

You have taken your audience on a journey from where they were at before the conversation to where they are headed because of the conversation. As you conclude the talk, end on a high note. Because the closing is the part that the audience remembers the most, make it strong and memorable, using many of the techniques in this book.

This chapter focuses on a few specific closing techniques. Oh, by the way, don't forget to end on time.

Early on in my career, I heard Ambassador Vernon Walters close his presentation with this sage advice: "I must go now while you still want me to stay." Even if they are hanging on your every word, do *not* go over time. Ever. It's about honoring your commitment to them; going over time is the most obvious and easiest way to disengage them.

73 SUMMARIZE KEY MESSAGES

You can have an amazing conversation, but if the audience doesn't do anything as a result, why bother? Tease out the key nuggets in the final few minutes of the panel discussion. Consider these ideas:

MODERATOR SUMMARIZE. Take a look at your notes and transition statements to summarize the discussion. Make sure you include one or two sentences about each panelist's contributions.

PANELISTS SUMMARIZE. Ask the panelists to summarize the session by asking for:

- *Final Thought.* Offer each panelist a last opportunity to share a key point, what the panelist is taking away from the conversation.

- *The One Thing.* Ask each panelist for the one thing they hope the audience takes away from the conversation.

- *Future-Forward.* Ask a question about the topic's future such as, "What important new trend will we be talking about at next year's conference?" "Where do you think we will be in five years?"

AUDIENCE SUMMARIZES. If you have a little time, why not ask the audience to summarize the session? Encourage the audience to think about what they heard and how it fits in with what they already know. Ask if there were any surprises or insights.

- *Shout Out.* Ask the audience to shout out what they consider to be the most important point(s) made and how they can personally apply the information.

- *What's Your Plan?* Ask your audience to talk with the person(s) sitting to the left and/or right about the most meaningful point(s) that are most applicable to their work, and how they will apply the information when they get back to the workplace. Debrief the small group conversation.

- *Combo.* After the moderator and/or panelists summarize, ask the audience, "So, what are you going to do about this?" Solicit some answers from a few audience members.

Do a roll call of the panelists, asking specifically for their takeaways.
Put the audience into breakout rooms to discuss their takeaways.
Call on a few willing participants.
Use the chatbox to note what they will do as a result of the discussion.
Curate their comments and send them to all participants.

END WITH A CALL TO ACTION 74

This is the crucial point where the cup meets the lip. You can have a great panel discussion, but if you haven't shifted the audience's perspective, increased their knowledge, or inspired them to do something differently, your words are for naught. Your audience will not take action unless you ask them to. Don't assume they know what they should do as a result of this brilliant conversation. It might be something as simple as asking them to consider the new ideas. Or you may want them to implement the new ideas immediately.

You need to top off your panel discussion with an explicit request, or you might ask the participants to share what they are going to do as a result of this session.

EXPLICIT REQUEST. Salespeople are always encouraged to ask for the sale. Make a similar request of your audience. What do you want them to *do*? Suggest a relatively easy action they could do when they get back to their offices. Ask them to do that easy action or make a more challenging request.

DO IT NOW. Get them to take the first step *in the room*. It might be something as simple as signing a form to express their interest or to tell the person sitting next to them what they will do.

RHETORICAL + DECLARATIVE. With a rhetorical question, you are getting emotional agreement. The declarative allows the participants to recognize real action can result. For example: "Can we do this? Yes, we can. We must do..."

REFLECTION. At the beginning of your presentation, encourage participants to write their special ideas or revelations on a notepad, sticky note, or their handout as they listen and participate. Toward the end of your speech, create a quiet space during which your participants can review what they jotted down and reflect on what they heard and learned.

ACTION PLAN. Ask the group to create their action plan; meaningful next steps as a result of the discussion and key takeaways. Some closing questions include:

- What is the one thing that you want to change in the next three months as a result of the information you heard today?

- What are you going to do differently based on what you've learned? What three things are going to move you closer to your goal?

- What will your first action step be as a result of today's event? How will you reward yourself for completing this action?

75   GIVE A REWARD

Rewards are powerful. Perhaps you can offer an incentive to the audience to be engaged.

As with any reward system, think about the behaviors you want to inspire: the audience to be engaged? Show up? Participate? Then think about an appropriate reward for that behavior. If at all possible, try to tie it into the topic.

Consider these ideas to reward the audience:

- One meeting organizer routinely hides a bucket of iced beer (or soft drinks) back stage to give to the table that interacts the most with the panelists.
- You could have a raffle with a prize related to the topic and they must be present to win.
- A prize for the first person who yells "bingo!" (if playing the game).
- A reward for the first person who asks a question during the Q&A segment.
- Give a prize to the brave soul who offers to be in the hot seat.
- Plan the panel at the end of the day so the audience wins a happy hour for staying engaged.

Rewarding the panelists is a bit trickier as it *could* reward odd behavior. For example, if you want to reward a panelist who gets the most tweets, you might have that person continually saying "Tweet this" which is just annoying. So decide whether you are going to tell the panelists about these potential awards:

- The Headliner Award for the panelist with the most memorable soundbite.
- The Storyteller Award for the panelist with the best story.
- The Tweety Award for the panelist who got the most tweets.
- The Chatty Award for the panelist who was most conversational.
- The Congeniality Award for the panelist who was the most courteous to the other panelists.

Show a visual representation of the prize, hold it up for all to see and share how you are going to get it to them. (email? Snail mail?). Make sure you actually *send it out* after the session. A reward could be a summary of the questions or the notes emailed to everyone after the session if they stay the whole session.

CREATE ACCOUNTABILITY 76

You asked your audience to revisit key messages and they identified a few meaningful steps forward. You can create an accountability structure that supports the participants' desire to follow up on their commitments. After all, how many times do we leave a presentation with good intentions and then get caught up in the urgencies of each day?

PUBLIC PROCLAMATION. Allow the opportunity for your participants to declare in front of their peers what they will do. You can do this with a show of hands or go around the room and ask, "What's the one thing you are committed to doing as a result of this presentation?" Once people make a public proclamation of their intent, there is a greater probability they'll complete it because they know that someone in that room might hold them accountable.

WRITE IT DOWN. Ask your audience to write their commitments on a blank 3"x5" index card. You can preprint the cards with a specific call to action. For example, "Here are three things I will do as a result of being part of this panel discussion."

ACCOUNTABILITY BUDDY. Ask the audience to find a partner with whom to share their commitment. It's best to pair up in groups of two; possibly three, but no more. The buddies exchange written commitments and contact information. (Get those business cards ready.) They agree to touch base at an agreed-upon interval (once a week or once a month) until the item is completed.

Some of the ways you can encourage accountability buddies include:

- Ask participants to simply shake hands with a buddy, exchange business cards, and make a solemn vow to follow up in a month.

- Have everyone write their commitments on a preprinted index card and exchange it with the accountability buddy: "I promise to call (accountability partner) on (date) and report my progress on (key thing each will do) as a result of the session." Signatures, email addresses, and phone numbers go on the cards.

- Provide preprinted multi-copy forms on which the participants write down their action plan. They keep the original form, a copy can go to the buddy, and you can keep another copy to enable you follow up and to provide the meeting organizer with your compiled results.

Even though you can't ask the participants to shake hands with a buddy, you **can** ask them to take a look at the participant list and ask them to send a private chat invitation to an accountability buddy. Once they agree, ask them to connect within the next 24 hours to chat about their commitments.

77 RAPID-FIRE LIGHTNING ROUND

Success Magazine Publisher, Darren Hardy, finished his interview with Marie Forleo and Robert Herjavec with "Rapid Fire Questions for off-the-cuff responses to have a little fun, get greater insight into who you are and what might be interesting for others to learn about you."

What a great idea to finish your panel discussion with a Rapid-Fire Lightning Round. Here are some of the questions they asked:

- If you were a box of cereal, what would you be and why?
- If you could sing one song on American Idol, what would it be?
- If you're on an island and could only bring three things with you, what would you bring?
- Do you believe in Bigfoot?
- If you were 80 years old, what would you tell your children about life and about business that would be the most important thing for them to know to get a head start?
- Three favorite books of all time?
- Most influential person in your life you are not related to?
- What cheers you up?
- Why do you invest in personal development?
- How do you define success?

You may also be familiar with James Lipton, host of the television show Inside the Actors' Studio. He always ended his interview with the *same* questions and then opened it up to audience Q&A:

- What is your favorite word?
- What is your least favorite word?
- What turns you on?
- What turns you off?
- What sound or noise do you love?
- What sound or noise do you hate?
- What profession other than your own would you like to attempt?
- What profession would you not like to do?

Pick a handful or come up with your own.

> You'll need to drive the rapid-fire pace by clarifying the directions and then calling on each panelist in quick succession.

THE 30 SECOND RANT 78

Here's a fun way to end your panel discussion: let your panelists go on a 30 second rant!

Let your panelists know that this is how you are going close the session. You're not asking them to script their response, but you coach them by saying, "At the end of the panel discussion, I'm going to let you go off on anything you want about this topic. You can rant, you can rave, but you have only 30 seconds to get it out. And you will be timed."

When you get to the end of the panel, say "It's time! I promised that you can go on a rant for exactly 30 seconds. I'll start the timer and give you a three-second countdown at the end. Panelist #1. Ready, set, go!"

When all the panelists have ranted, thank them, and you're done with your panel discussion.

79 CLOSE WITH A GROUP ACTIVITY

A panel discussion ain't over until it's over. Why not punctuate your panel with a group activity to discuss what just happened? Here are three ways you can involve the audience in the conversation:

1. **EASIEST.** At the conclusion of the discussion, ask the participants to form small groups to discuss:
   - Key points that struck them or had an impact.
   - Key points that are most applicable to their life.
   - What questions they still have.
   - The implications they are drawing from the panel conversation.

   After the groups discuss it for a few minutes, ask for some findings/questions from each group (or from a few selected groups). This is easiest if you can have the room set in round tables.

2. **HARDER.** At the conclusion of the panelists' discussion, designate a predetermined discussion topic for each table (if set in table rounds) OR invite people to get up and go to a table that has the predetermined topic they are interested in or invite people to get up and go to a designated space in the room that has a predetermined topic posted on a flipchart hanging on the wall. Panelists can be invited to join a group where a relevant topic is being discussed.

   Optional brief reflections from the tables can be shared with the whole group at the end.

3. **HARDEST.** Prior to the discussion, ask each small group to brainstorm issues related to the panel topic. It's handy, but not imperative to give each group a piece of paper on which to list their brilliant ideas. Each group then identifies their top three issues, writes them on a 4"x 6" index card, and hands the index card to you, the moderator.

   The moderator collects all the cards and identifies themes, then uses the information to structure the panel discussion.

   At the conclusion of the session, bookend the panel with a small group discussion on how to deal with those issues. Ask the same small groups to brainstorm suggestions about how to deal with the identified issue. Ask them to narrow their ideas down to the top three, write them on an index card, and hand the card to the moderator. The results can then be compiled and delivered to the organization to consider or to assign to a task force or to take immediate action.

> Place the participants into predetermined or randomly selected breakout rooms to discuss the topic.

WRAP UP THE CONVERSATION 80

Rattling off housekeeping reminders can be awfully dull. With a little bit of foresight, you can make them quick *and* compelling:

BEST CONTACT INFO. Let the panelists share where they can be found online or where others can learn more about them. Model the final statement for them as, "I work at [company] in [job title] role. I can be found online at [URL]." Each panelist could have a stack of business cards available for participants to take on their way out.

EXTEND THE CONVERSATION. Invite the audience to extend the conversation in the front of the room, in the hallway or in the bookstore immediately after the end of the session. You can also encourage the discussion to move online to the conference website, blog, wiki, forum or social media platform groups such as Facebook or LinkedIn. Share any additional resources available to the attendees. Encourage any photographers to post their pictures.

PROMOTIONAL KICKER. Allow panelists to let the audience know something about them or their company, such as when an upcoming product release will be.

THANK YOU. Quickly thank the audience, conference sponsors, meeting chair or planner, A/V crew and each panelist by name.

GIFTS. If there are gifts for the panelists, have them *ready* to hand out or show the audience one of the gifts that you'll give each panelist after the session is over. You can present the gift to each panelist right then and there or immediately after the panel.

FINAL ANNOUNCEMENTS such as location of the next activity following the panel. Alert the audience to upcoming events, future programs, handouts, evaluation forms, educational credit forms and other details as necessary.

Finally, ask the audience to join you in expressing appreciation for such a brilliant panel discussion with their applause.

Start clapping and the audience will clap, too.

81 TAKE IT INTO THE HALLWAY

So what happens immediately after the panel discussion? People hover around the panelists wanting to ask a specific question. What about everyone else? What if they want to keep talking but, as in most cases, the room needs to be turned during the break?

Take a cue from American Society of Association Executive's Great Ideas Conference where they set up some bar height tables with mini chalkboards describing discussion topics in the common areas—and then encouraged people to congregate around those topics. Since ASAE's theme was on creativity, innovation, and reinvention, they also placed creative puzzles and toys on the tables to engage the mind.

You can do this too. Think about how you want the participants to stay engaged in the conversation immediately after your panel discussion. You might want to use mini-chalkboards and ask your panelists to go mingle near the chalkboards.

At the very least, stick around. Listen to what the participants say. It's a great indicator of panel success.

> Since there isn't a hallway to gather in, keep the virtual meeting room open for further discussion.
> Offer to place the participants into breakout rooms for further discussion if they wish.
>
> BTW, unless they are used to this practice, or you have mentioned it often enough, people will not ask to do this.

CONTINUE THE CONVERSATION 82

Congratulations! You moderated an amazingly successful panel discussion. You delivered on the promise, made the panelists look like heroes and the audience received tremendous value. But it's not over yet. Here are ten things you can do to continue the conversation *and* build credibility with the audience and meeting organizers:

SEEK OUT OTHERS. For the remainder of the conference, seek out people who were highly engaged and connect with them sometime during the conference. You'll build some great relationships.

QUESTION CARDS. Collect question cards and coordinate responses from the panelists. Feed the answers into the organization's newsletter, FAQs or other communication vehicles.

CRITIQUE. Within 24 hours after the session, make a few notes about what you liked and what you might do differently the next time you moderate a panel discussion.

DEBRIEF. Chat with the meeting chair/planner about the session. Review evaluation forms. Ask if there was anything they would have liked you to do differently so you can do a better job next time.

THANK YOUS. Send a personal note, card, or email to each panelist, the meeting coordinator and anyone else who made your life easier. Thank them for doing such a great job adding something specific about what they did or said that contributed to the panel's success.

KEEP YOUR PROMISES. If you or your panelists promised to get the name of a great book, research the answer to a question, or send a related article, then do it as soon as you can.

SUMMARY REPORT. Using your notes and Twitter feed, provide a written summary of the panel discussion to the meeting chair that includes:

- Short description of the panel along with panelist names and estimated audience size.
- Brief summary of the discussion and conclusions.
- Recommendations for future panels.

REPURPOSE YOUR SUMMARY. Take tidbits of wisdom from your summary and:

- Post the highlights, key quotes and photos on the event website or social media.
- Post the slides on Slideshare.net.
- Write a blog about your experience.
- Share the summary with key clients and potential customers.

RECORDINGS. The meeting organizer may post the professional audio, video, or transcript file for others to access or post your own recording with their permission. Provide links and take excerpts from the transcript to use in follow-up communications to panelists and post-conference communications.

KEEP LEARNING. Review your own performance. Watch others. Attend other conferences to observe how different people moderate. Learn what works for them and what doesn't. Integrate your learning into each subsequent panel you moderate or participate in.

> Make sure you save the question and chatbox comments.
> This is a wealth of information to repurpose to extend the conversation.

CASE STUDY
CONTINUOUS IMPROVEMENT

The main way to learn how to add more pizazz to your panel is to moderate more frequently. Note what works and what doesn't work. Keep doing what works well and change the things that don't work as well. I realize how basic this sounds, but I'm continually surprised at how seldom this happens.

Here's what typically happens. You moderate the panel and then dash off to the next assignment. While you are driving, you think about what worked well and what you would do next time. And you *think* you will remember your observations. But you don't moderate another panel for another few weeks (or months), and when it rolls around, you've forgotten all the things you wanted to do differently.

If you really want to improve your panel moderation skills, go the extra mile and formally critique yourself:

REFLECT. As soon as possible after your session, take a moment to reflect on what went well and what did not go so well. Review your working agenda and note where you followed the agenda and where you deviated.

ANALYZE. Ask yourself these two questions:
- "Why did that technique work?"
- "Why didn't that activity work as well as I thought it would?"

Your answers have a host of causes ranging from technique selection to your comfort level to the actual content to the audience's personality.

UPGRADE. How would you improve the panel the next time? Write down specifics about how you would change it.

ONE THING. Close to the bottom of the working agenda, draw a red line across the page. Write down the major thing you learned through this critique process. It could be something you want to reinforce or change for the next time.

RATE YOURSELF. Give yourself a realistic grade on a scale of 1 to 5 (with 1 being the lowest and 5 being the highest) for the overall panel as well as each category technique. Any grade below a 5 is an opportunity for improvement.

FILE. Place your annotated working agenda in a Continuous Improvement binder or digital file folder. Periodically, flip through it to see themes, patterns, and trends as well as specific improvements.

PART THREE

KEEP THE AUDIENCE

INTERESTED

IN A

PANEL DISCUSSION

CHAPTER TEN
SHIFT GEARS

Let's say your panels last 60 to 90 minutes. For your audience, that's an eternity! They crave a mental break, a shot of energy, a short (and pleasant) detour. Give it to them and you'll be rewarded with an even more engaged audience!

~ Brad Montgomery

THE BEST WAY to keep the conversation moving and the audience engaged is to shift gears every six to ten minutes.

Why every six to ten minutes?

Because that's the attention span of the average adult. We are so used to television commercials popping up every ten minutes, it is no wonder our minds start to drift.

When you've covered the first topic enough, don't be afraid to break the monotony. Shake it up. Change the tempo of the traditional, ho-hum boring panel discussion.

Although this entire book is full of ideas to shift gears and add more pizazz to your panel, this chapter is devoted to specific ideas to help you shift gears *during* the session to keep the audience on the edge of their seats.

83 IMPROV TECHNIQUE

The improv technique is a lively way to *start* a panel discussion (see Tip #48—Switch! An Improv Opening) and also an excellent way to shift gears *during* a panel discussion:

Take one of your carefully crafted questions and tell the panelists that they must add to what has been said by saying, "Yes and..."

Start with the person the farthest away from you and then go down the line until it gets to you. Then say something witty or open it up to a conversation about what was said.

For example, you might ask, "What are some of the challenges you see ahead [about the topic]? We'll start with panelist A (who is sitting the farthest away from you) and then each of you must improv it by saying, 'Yes and...'"

It's a quick way of getting the ideas out on the table during your panel discussion.

> Because the panelists are not literally sitting next to each other,
> they will not know the order of the lineup unless you tell them.
> Ask them to keep their microphones on and tell them their lineup.
> Repeat the question and let the improv begin.
> Don't be surprised if you have to cue the next person to talk
> by simply stating their first name.

PROGRESSIVE ANSWERS 84

Have you ever seen the game Pillars? If you have, that's great, if not, it may take you a minute more to appreciate this improv technique of progressive answers.

You, as the moderator, ask a panelist an interesting question. I like to do this from one of the questions submitted by an audience member, but any question will do. At any time during the panelist's answer, you yell "Pause!" and then point to another panelist, who picks up the answer where the previous panelist left off. Stop the answers at a logical conclusion—in other words, when it's been answered.

Repeat with one or two more questions as long as it is interesting and relevant. No more than three times because the panelists and the audience get tired of repeating the same technique. Remember to switch gears again during your panel discussion.

> With this technique, pointing to a panelist is pointless.
> Firmly and loudly state "Pause! [name of next panelist]. Go!"

85 PANELIST ASKS THE QUESTION

Want to really shift gears, throw a wrench into an otherwise traditional panel discussion? Ask one of your panelists to ask a question to a specific audience member.

That's right. Pick one panelist to select one audience member (known or unknown to the panelist, doesn't matter) and have the panelist ask that audience member a question.

The question can be a poll, a query for more information, or just a random question: "Are you having a good day today?" Regardless, it creates curiosity in the crowd, and makes them lean forward, thinking, "Ok, at any point they could call me out!"

Only do this once or twice. Maybe three times tops. Otherwise, the audience might highjack your session.

Tell the audience you are going to unmute the person whose name is called. The audience will be thinking, "Oh no! I better pay attention!"

You can even ham it up a bit asking the panelist, "Who are you going to pick?" Just make sure that you, the ombudsman, or the technician, quickly unmutes that person.

Otherwise, it will feel like forever for the person to unmute themselves.

RAPID-FIRE PANELIST POLLING 86

Here's another technique to shift gears and change the pace: Take a rapid-fire poll of the panelists.

There are a few ways you can do this:

RATE FROM 1-10. Ask each of the panelists, on a scale of 1–10, 1 being the lowest and 10 being the highest, how they would rate _____ (pick an issue). They MUST pick a number, don't let them go into explaining why. It should be quick and easy. After all panelists have weighed in, you can make an observational comment ("Wow! We have a wide range here!"), decide to probe deeper into one panelist's response, or continue with your next poll.

YES / NO / MAYBE. Create an interesting closed question such as "Do you think this [future trend] is going to happen in the next five years? Yes, no, or maybe?" *Note: I've known some to switch the "maybe" to "It's Complicated." That's up to you.*

FIVER. In this poll, ask a question to the panelists and they must answer in five words (and it must be five words only). Encourage your panelists to use their fingers because it gets quite stressful, edgy, and fun! It's also revelatory. They must be able to show brilliance in five words, in the moment, counting on their fingers while a bazillion people are staring at them. *Note: there's no face loss to struggle a little bit because everyone has placed themselves vicariously in the panelists' position. They are thinking "What would I do?"*

IS IT BETTER? This poll requires panelists to answer quickly. Think of two things you know the organization doesn't have complete agreement on. You want to know which side of the fence the panelists are on.

THE ONE BREATH RULE. Ask the panelists a question and they can answer as long as they want in one breath. What normally happens when you are describing this new ground rule is they won't believe you. So when the first panelist starts to answer the question and takes his first breath, you must jump in. Just watch the rest of the panelists go *"Whaaaaat?"* The second panelist starts to panic and you'll see the audience lean in to see what happens next.

With these rapid-fire polling techniques, you could rattle through a lot of questions and get a lot of interesting engagement from all panelists in a very short period of time.

Because the panelists are not literally sitting next to each other,
they will not normally know the order of the lineup unless you tell them.
Ask them to keep their microphones on and remind them of the lineup.
Repeat the question and let the polling begin.
Don't be surprised if you have to cue the next person to talk
by simply stating their first name.

87 AGREE/DISAGREE GAME

Want to break up a rather mundane panel discussion? Try polling panelists with the agree/disagree game.

When the audience is large (over 300), and you only have a short amount of time, try breaking it up about two-thirds of the way with the Agree/Disagree Game. Here's how it works:

The moderator says, "Let's play a game: Agree/Disagree. Each of our panelists has an agree/disagree paddle. I'm going to make a statement that may be provocative for the purpose of discussion. Then each of our panelists can agree or disagree with that statement. Let's start by testing the paddles to make sure they work."

Make the first statement. For example, "This panel is, hands down, no holds barred, the very best panel with the best looking panelists you've ever seen in the entire universe."

Cue laughter! And the panelists use their agree/disagree paddles to vote.

"Now that we have the hang of this, let's continue with another harder and more serious question."

Then ask three or four more questions that you believe will have polarizing answers or will inspire an interesting conversation that the audience will literally lean in to hear. After each question, allow the panelists to explain their answers. If necessary, ask probing follow-up questions to inspire the conversation during your scintillating panel discussion.

> Make sure your panelists have an agree/disagree paddle.
> Either mail it to them or have them create their own.

POP QUIZ 88

At the *Evolution of Private Debt Funds* panel at the CREF conference, moderator Jack Cohen, CEO of Darkknight Ventures, injected some levity into the discussion in the form of some light-hearted pop quizzes:

THREE WORDS OR LESS. Panelists were asked to describe the current alternative lending environment in three words or less. "Very competitive," said panelist Jimmy Yung, a managing director at Blackstone Real Estate Debt Strategies; "Seeing some cracks," panelist Greta Guggenheim, CEO of TPG Real Estate Finance Trust, opined; "Too much capital," said Tom MacManus, the president of A10 Capital.

THE 12-YEAR-OLD TEST. Panelists were asked to define a debt fund's role in terms that even a 12-year-old would understand. Yung was given a gold star by Cohen for offering this simple definition: "We give people money to buy properties and ask them to pay us back."

You can do a pop quiz too, but you'll need to think about them ahead of time. Trust me; it's not easy to dream these up in the moment! For inspiration, check out trivia games or conversation starters and adopt those questions to your topic. You're bound to come up with some interesting pop quiz questions.

For example, I picked up the book *The Conversation Piece: Creative Questions to Tickle the Mind* by Bret Nicholaus and Paul Lowrie. I opened it up and landed on question #95: "The year is 2050; having a grass lawn is a thing of the past. What might have replaced the green stuff?" What a great question that we can adapt to our panel: "The year is 2050; having _____ is a thing of the past. What might have replaced it?"

As you share the directions for your pop quiz, ask all panelists to unmute themselves and share the order they should respond.
Ask the audience to participate in the pop quiz in their chatbox.

89   SHOW A SHORT VIDEO CLIP

Want to start your panel discussion with a bang? With drama? With emotion? Or, switch gears using a video snippet—a quick, short video clip that reinforces the panel's key message. A minute or less is about right (just a snippet); otherwise, you risk losing your audience's attention. For example, I saw a panel moderator use a video clip of legendary golfer Tiger Woods chipping into the hole from the rough grass—and it barely dropped in—as a metaphor for hitting your goal against all odds. It took all of 15 seconds and captivated the audience. The moderator then used that metaphor to start the discussion.

So where do you get these short video snippets?

YOUTUBE. A ton of engaging videos can be found at this site with the implied consent of the copyright holder to redistribute the video. That means you can reuse the video in your presentation as long as it is still posted on the site. So check the site each time you plan to use the clip; the license terminates within a "commercially reasonable amount of time" once the work is removed from the website.

MOVIE/TV CLIPS. Most audiences perk up when you use a short video clip from a popular movie. Again, be advised, when you use a video in a public meeting or training environment (regardless of whether you are profit or a nonprofit organization), it is considered a public performance and requires the consent of the original copyright holder or its agent. To obtain information, permission, and/or purchase rights to use movie clips, contact Motion Picture Licensing Corporation (www.mplc.com) or Audio Cine Films Inc. (www.acf-film.com).

YOUR OWN. As you are doing research for your panel, take your video camera and film the audience in action at an earlier event, interview rising stars or celebrities around the topic, or dig up some interesting visuals. Splice the best of the best into one short video. (By the way, you thought you could get rid of the lawyers this way, right? Wrong. If you plan on broadcasting your video to the larger world in a profit or not-for-profit environment, save yourself a headache and get each person's written consent to be in your video at the time you do the filming.)

PURCHASE CLIPS. You can purchase video clips that announce breaks, open or close a session, or provide a lighthearted moment. Typically, when you purchase the video, you also purchase the legal right to use it in a public setting. But check to be certain.

CUSTOM VIDEO. Plenty of resources are available to customize video for your presentation. It gets a bit pricey, so practice due diligence and do a dry run of how you are going to use the clip before you actually commission the production.

Every platform has its own unique eccentricities. Please do a dry run to make sure your video is able to be seen and heard by all.

LIGHTNING ROUND 90

Change up the format by inserting a lightning round of quick questions with your panelists—especially when you have more than five panelists.

So what, exactly is a lightning round? It is a QUICK questioning of the panel. You can either ask it to all panelists or a different question to each panelist, but one right after the other. Boom, boom, boom!

The key to making this technique work is in the preparation: ALL of the questions need to thoughtful and intentional. Phrase them concisely so it forces the panelist to answer with a word, phrase or sentence at the most. Best to have them on index cards so you can rifle right through them.

For example, let's say you are moderating a panel about XYZ topic. At the beginning of the panel, you could ask, "What's the one thing that drives you crazy about XYZ?" or "What do you adore about XYZ?" Similarly, at the end, you could ask, "If there's one thing you want people to remember as a result of our conversation here today, what would it be?" Or, sometime in between, ask, "What's the one thing you would do to solve this issue/problem?"

It's best to use a lightning round when you want crisp, defined comments from panelists. The key to using this technique is to announce, "And now it's time for a lightning round!" This creates a bit of energy and anticipation and the audience is thinking, "Okay, this is something new!"

Explain the rules of the lightning round. For example, "I'm going to ask a series of questions (three is a nice number) and the panelists will answer with one or no more than two sentences—absolutely no more. This is meant to be a LIGHTNING ROUND where the answers should come quickly. Ready panelists?"

Then follow the process strictly. Using a lightning round is a great way to mix it up, keep the energy high, and help panelists focus their comments.

Because the panelists are not literally sitting next to each other, they will not know the order of the lineup unless you tell them. Ask them to keep their microphones on and tell them their lineup. Repeat the question and let the first panelist answer the question.

Don't be surprised if you have to cue the next person to talk by simply stating their first name.

91   INJECT SPONTANEITY

Want your panel discussion to be memorable? Maybe even have a viral moment at the conference? The trick is to have the moderator or panelists do something unexpected, usually spontaneous. Something you can't get on YouTube. Something you wouldn't normally witness in one of your organization's typical panel discussions.

When I mention this to my clients, I usually hear silence. A cough. Then a hesitant question, "*Ummm...how do I do that?*"

There is such a thing as planned spontaneity where a panelist plans to do something that actually *appears* to be spontaneous in the eyes of the audience. But it's really not. The panelist has actually prepared for the moment. For example: a client was a panelist at a very prominent convention. He knew he would be asked a technical question about an upcoming product release. He thought, "Wouldn't it be cool to call the lead developer while looking like it was a spontaneous idea?" To prepare, he made sure the developer was available by cell during the entire time of the panel—and the developer would keep her answers crisp and clear. He also confirmed with the A/V crew about the technical details to projecting the developers' audio. In this case the microphone was placed directly on the phone. He tried it out during a dry run. *Guess what?* The question came up during the panel discussion. He said, "Hey, why don't I just call the lead developer and get it straight from her?" The audience then got to hear firsthand details.

The ability to pull off planned spontaneity is largely dependent on the panelists' personal style and confidence that it will be interesting and benefit the audience.

- It *should* relate to the topic. But not all the time. Sometimes, a small distraction can be welcome.
- Make it culturally appropriate for the audience. Don't do something that will just piss them off.
- Panelists: It's helpful to give the meeting organizer and moderator a heads up on your intentions.

Encourage your panelists to brainstorm ideas on their own, or join in a brainstorming session with just one panelist, or hold a brainstorming session with all the panelists. The point is to put the seed of inspiration in their heads. It just ain't going to happen on its own.

You have to be intentional. The most remarkable moments are actually well thought out. Sometimes even rehearse it so you know it will go well. If it works, run with it. And if it bombs (which it might), simply move on. No harm, no foul.

Then again, you don't have to plan everything out. Encourage your panelists to look for moments of spontaneous human kindness. Actor Chris Evans was on a panel at the 2019 ACE Comic-con in Seattle. They were in the middle of the audience Q&A segment when Evans spied an adorable dog in the front row disguised as Iron Man. Guess what? He jumped off the stage to pet the dog! Matzav Review reported, "On Twitter and on the site all their fans went crazy, especially when you hear the emotion in his voice when he said: Hello, friend!"

Now that's a purely spontaneous memorable moment!

SURPRISE APPEARANCE 92

If you would like to add a sense of awe and buzz in the halls at your next panel discussion, consider having a "surprise" guest—a well-known personality with celebrity status from the audience's perspective. (Of course, to the meeting organizer, it won't be a surprise, but to the audience, and perhaps the panelists, it will be!)

Here are four primary ways to have your celebrities surprise the audience:

1. **UNANNOUNCED.** The guest can be an unannounced panelist introduced at the beginning along with all the other panelists.

2. **POP IN.** The guest can join the panel after it has started. For example, E! Online reported that "Harrison Ford popped up unexpectedly at the *Stars Wars: The Force Awakens* panel...like it was nothing. But it was *so* something. His arrival, which received a standing ovation from the 6,000 people who waited forever to get into Hall H, marked the actor's first official public appearance since he was injured in a plane crash in March."

3. **IN THE AUDIENCE.** You can also have your surprise guest out in the audience and ask the panel a question. Bill Nye, the Science Guy, surprised Congresswoman Alexandria Ocasio-Cortez (AOC) at the South by Southwest (SXSW) panel. Irene Fagan Merro reported that "perhaps the most memorable moment was...when the moderator turned to the audience for questions, Bill Nye approached the mic to ask the freshman House Rep his own [question]." She continued, "Bill Nye addressing AOC as if he is any other attendee was extremely refreshing and sincere. AOC agreed, as she gave him a standing ovation of her own after he asked his question."

4. **DRIVE BY.** Finally, you can do a drive by where the surprise guest can be included via live or recorded video to share a short insight at the beginning, middle, or end of your panel discussion.

93   USE A PROP

Have you ever thought about using a prop to help shift gears during a panel discussion? I have, ever since I saw Sally Hogshead drag out a bottle of Jägermeister at the National Speakers Association Annual Convention. (See Case Study at end of this chapter.)

A prop can be used at the beginning of a panel (see Tip #55—Show and Tell) or any time you or your panelists want to strengthen the audience's ability to visualize, understand, accept, and remember an idea, concept, or theme during the panel discussion.

HOW TO USE A PROP

STEP 1   KEEP IT HIDDEN
Keep the prop out of sight until you're ready to use it—unless you want to keep the prop onstage to arouse curiosity.

STEP 2   AGREE
Ask the audience to agree with you on an idea that is connected to the prop. Get them to nod.

STEP 3   INTRODUCE PROP
Introduce the prop to the audience. Hold it in front of you; hold it high and hold it steady. Move it slowly so it can be seen from all parts of the room. Do not talk to the prop. Talk to the audience.

STEP 4   SHARE THE PROP
Don't hesitate to share the prop with your panelists—even with the audience (if it's not too fragile or valuable).

STEP 5   PUT IT AWAY
Put it away or out of sight when you're done. Resist the temptation to pass it around. The handoff from person to person and each person's close inspection will be very distracting.

> The audience should be able to see the entire prop within their field of vision of your camera. If they need to see detail, you need to hold it close to the camera. Or share your screen to show a picture of the prop.

See how Sally Hogshead used this technique in the case study at the end of this chapter.

MORPH THE TOPIC 94

Have you ever been on a panel (or watched one) when the topic started out in one direction, and because of the synergy of the panelists as well as the interest and energy of the audience, the conversation morphed in a different direction?

Yes, it happens. Sometimes it's a good shift because the panel discussion should benefit the audience. If the conversation isn't getting there, then you gotta shift. Then again, the conversation might have been hijacked by some panelists or a few vocal and visual audience members. What do you do?

I call this a strategic moment when the moderator has a choice. The moderator can continue on the prescribed path or proceed in the new direction.

Strategic moments are both a crisis and an opportunity. The crisis is one of faith. If the moderator calls a new direction, will the audience agree (or slam them on the session evaluation)? If the moderator chooses a new path, will that conversation be lively and informative? It will certainly be spontaneous, but will it still meet the needs of the audience?

When facing a strategic moment, the panel moderator needs to:

MAKE A CONSCIOUS CHOICE. The moderator is in a quandary. What to do? Whatever you decide, make an intentional choice. If left undecided, panelists and audience will be confused and the conversation will become scattered.

CALL IT. Recognize that the panel is facing a strategic moment where the discussion will diverge from the advertised objective of the panel. Make sure everyone (panelists and audience) understands the significance of the moment.

DECLARE A NEW PATH. Since the conversation is going to go in a new direction, describe the process—*how* you are going to proceed. Most of the time, the *process* will not change, just the focus and *content* of the conversation.

CHECK FOR AGREEMENT. Look for the nodding of heads or raising of hands before you boldly move to the new focus. Even though *everyone* may not be in agreement, as long as you have the majority, you'll be able to move forward.

When faced with a strategic moment, make a conscious choice to change direction, announce it to the panelists and audience, then declare the process you'll use to continue the conversation.

95 RIP UP YOUR CARDS

What happens when the speaker that tees up the panel discussion doesn't talk about the designated topic? Yep. It happens more often than I care to admit. The host, sponsor, or presenter, for whatever reason, chooses to deviate from the objectives printed in the conference program. Hopefully, the presentation was still an intriguing, provocative presentation—just not what the moderator had planned.

So what would you do as the moderator?

You essentially have two choices:

1. **STAY WITH YOUR MODERATED QUESTIONS.** It will probably be an okay discussion that comes off a little disjointed and awkward. Definitely not the homerun your meeting organizers were hoping for.

2. **RIP UP YOUR QUESTIONS.** Walk out with your moderated question cards and ripped them up in front of the audience. Since the presenter went off script, so must the panel. The show must go on!

Start with the big takeaway question: "What was your biggest Ah-Ha or takeaway from the presentation?" or be a little more daring, "What did you find yourself in disagreement on with our speaker today?"

The moderator is the champion for the audience, making segues and transitions so the audience gets real value from the conversation. Sometimes, your carefully crafted plan just isn't going to work. That's when you fall back to Plan B—your secondary plan for the unlikely event that something odd is going to happen.

Now, if an odd thing happens to the presentation that kicks off your panel discussion, you'll be prepared.

USE A PROP

Sally Hogshead hauled out a bottle of Jägermeister on stage at the National Speakers Association Annual Conference Influence 2011, (which you can view at https://youtu.be/L-QlaFxh8qA—fast forward about seven minutes in).

The panel topic was about branding, riffing off the TV Show *Real Time with Bill Maher*. But this time, it was *Real Time with Scott McKain* along with Brendon Burchard, Bill Bacharach, and Sally Hogshead.

Hogshead told a story about that notorious liquor brand, Jägermeister. She held up a bottle and asked, "It tastes like a mixture of kerosene and battery acid, right? Jager is the most popular brand nobody likes!" The audience applauded with grins on their faces.

Then, true to form, Hogshead pulled out four shot glasses and challenged the panel to take a shot! What a hoot!

Do you think she got our attention? Yep! Did she make her point? You bet! Am I still talking about nine years later? Check!

Afterward, I asked Hogshead about the decision to do this and if she gave anyone a heads up. Her answer? "I didn't tell anyone in advance, because I wanted it to be a surprise for the panel and the audience. But I did get the okay from Scott McKain while we were backstage, just to make sure I wasn't stepping on any toes."

Sure, she took a risk. But it was a well-calculated risk. As she says, "Different is better than better."

CHAPTER ELEVEN
ENGAGE THE AUDIENCE

Never do for the audience what they can do for themselves.

~ Bob Pike

TODAY'S AUDIENCES ARE DEMANDING more engagement and interaction—especially during a panel discussion format.

Nothing will turn them off more than lengthy introductions, followed by panelist presentations and then "Oops! Sorry, we don't have time for audience Q&A."

Rather than waiting for the end to engage an audience, why not engage them beforehand, as they walk into the room, at the beginning and throughout the entire panel session?

This chapter will give you all kinds of ideas to engage the audience.

96 ENGAGE BEFOREHAND

Imagine the types of people (even specific individuals as models) who are likely to attend. Preemptively ask some of the questions they are likely to ask. Find out what's on their minds, what would really wow them and keep them talking long after the meeting is over.

INTERVIEW A FEW PEOPLE who will be in the audience. Ask the conference organizer for the names and contact information for three influencers or heavy hitters who may be in the audience. Ask them what they would like to hear about and what challenges they're facing.

CHAT VIA SOCIAL MEDIA. Use the conference website, a blog post, Twitter, or other feedback tools to glean questions from the community. Ask them to submit their most pressing issues and challenges.

SEND AN EMAIL OR VOICEMAIL BLAST. Some organizations have the ability to blast a voicemail or email to all participants encouraging them to attend the session and submit their questions.

Start the conversation on those channels, encouraging them to come to the session. And don't forget that their input is invaluable when curating questions for the panel.

PROMOTE THE PANEL 97

It's sad, but true. No one really thinks about the moderator during the marketing and promotion process. Although, as a panel moderator, you are not directly responsible for marketing the program, you can certainly help meeting organizers promote the event, your panel session, and engage attendees.

When you are a moderator, try these ideas to tastefully and effectively assist with the marketing process before the panel session.

PROMOTIONAL MATERIALS. Take a look at the event app, promotional materials, and website. At the very least, there should be a catchy title with a summary of what the audience will get out of it. Panelist and moderator bios are helpful along with their Twitter usernames. If this information isn't there, work with the meeting organizer to get it in the program.

ALIGNMENT. Make sure the marketing materials and promotional promises match what you have planned for your agenda.

SOCIAL MEDIA. Let everyone know about the upcoming, wildly interesting, panel discussion through social media channels. Your blog, Twitter, LinkedIn, and Facebook accounts are all great ways to promote your panel ahead of time and to solicit questions from the audience.

SURVEY. Create a short web-based survey for the attendees to complete prior to attending the event, perhaps during the registration process. Solicit questions and other details that would make your panel discussion truly engaging for them.

TWITTER. Set up a Twitter hashtag to solicit questions ahead of time and from the audience during the event. *Note: if the event has two or more sessions going on at the same time with fervent Tweeters, you might see some conflicting threads in the Twitter stream.*

VIDEO. Create a video teaser explaining the objective of the panel and the caliber of the panelists.

INVITE OTHERS. Send promotional materials to clients, potential customers, and those you know who might be interested in attending the panel or event. Encourage your panelists to do likewise. After you moderate the panel, reach out to them again to let them know how it went. Share the key points.

One final word of caution when promoting the event: Make it about the event, the session, and the audience; not about you. Beware of flagrant self-promotion.

98 PERIODICALLY POLL THE AUDIENCE

Perhaps you polled the audience at the beginning of the panel … you can also poll them periodically during the session.

Gauge the room with a quick survey or quiz using a show of hands, thumbs up or down, stand up, make a noise, shout out, wave a flag or color-coded response card, raise your agree/disagree paddle etc. You can also use an audience response system, meeting app such as CrowdCompass by Cvent, a text-based app such as PollEverywhere, or a web-based app such as Slido.com.

Karen Hough, founder and CEO of ImprovEdge suggests, "One fun improvisational tip is to leverage a 'Yes' or 'No' topic. Ask the audience: 'Let's pause and see what our audience thinks of that. Raise your hand if you would have taken action. Great. Now raise your hand if you would have waited without taking action.' That involves the audience, and gives you fodder to comment on the panelist's story. 'Wow, John, less than half of our audience would have taken action as you did. Tell us how you summoned the courage to do so.'"

Your digital platform will have a polling feature.
You must either frontload the poll or create an instant poll.
However, depending on the size of the group, let your imagination run
with different, creative ways to take a poll.

Some ideas include:
Literally raise your hand if everyone is showing video
Raise a colored object that shows your choice
Use the "raise hand" functionality
Use your emotion buttons (thumbs up or clap hands)
Comment in the chatbox
Turn your sound on and make a noise

ASK FOR AN AUDIENCE RESPONSE 99

An easy way to get the audience engaged early on in your panel discussion is to ask for verbal responses. Preachers do this all the time: If you believe you're going to heaven, say, "Amen!" and the audience shouts "Amen!"

You could also ask the audience to say, "You Bet!" or exclaim "Oh Yeah!" or shout out "Uh-huh!" If confidentiality is important, ask for those who agree to hum. You'll find those who are passionate will hum loudly! No need to limit yourself to verbal responses, either. You can ask them to "Applaud if you like vanilla ice cream" or "Stand up if you are committed to making ice cream available all summer long."

On the flip side of the coin you can also ask the audience to say, "Oh No" shout out "No way" or even "Boo" if you don't like pistachio ice cream.

This is, in fact, a simplified version of polling. There is just one choice and one action which you believe the majority of the people in the audience are in agreement with. Equally as important to selecting the choice you want to poll is the response that they will actually give. People will say Hallelujah or Praise the Lord in a church, but will they willingly and loudly say it in front of peers? That's for you to decide.

Here are some examples of different types of autoresponders where you actually expect or train the audience to respond with a specific answer:

SING ALONGS. Think of a campfire sing-along (often a round). Have the audience follow and sing along with you.

REPEAT AFTER ME. Ask the group to make a pledge to you and their fellow participants as they commit to a new behavior. "I do solemnly swear..."

FILL-IN-THE-BLANK. Let the audience finish your sentence with an extremely well-known phrase or answer. Roxanne Emmerich, culture transformation specialist, tells a story about when she first moved to Minnesota and went shopping at the Mall of America. The shopkeepers would come up to her and say, "May I help you?" and her answer would always be "No, thank you. Just ____ (pause)." The participants were able to fill in each pause as she would lean forward with the expectation that they would chime in with the obvious answer.

EXPRESSIONS. Create a specific tag such as an expression or physical movement. Give the audience a solid visible or audible cue for when they should respond by doing something you've trained them to do. For example, when Tim Gard, a laugh-out-loud humorist, puts two thumbs up, the audience is trained to say, "Woo hoo," and when he puts his hand to his forehead, they know to say, "Bummer."

HEADLINES. Reduce your major points to headlines that your audience can easily recall or revisit when prompted. When Shep Hyken, an award-winning speaker on customer service, shares several examples of a moment of misery as opposed to a moment of magic, after a few stories, the audience is calling out whether it is a moment of magic or a moment of misery. You know you have a phrase that pays when they can recall your headline long after the panel.

Just keep in mind that the volume of the response can also show the strength of the audience's interest level and/or commitment. Which is handy information to have at the start of your panel or to poll periodically during your panel discussion.

HOW TO CREATE AN AUTORESPONDER

STEP 1   ASK
You have to ask for the group's permission. Jeff Tobe, a guru of innovation and change, asks his audiences to respond with an energetic ABSOLUTELY whenever they're in agreement with a question he asks the audience.

STEP 2   MODEL
Before you can expect the audience to follow you, model the behavior you want. Jeff shows them what an energetic ABSOLUTELY response sounds like. This is done in two places: during the request and in step #3.

STEP 3   AFFIRM
You can be patient and see if they pick up the mantra naturally, or you can ask for them to repeat it. Jeff simply asks, "Can you do that?" while leaning forward with the expectation that the audience will respond with the correct answer.

STEP 4   REINFORCE
When you get a strong response, acknowledge it. When it is rather wimpy (which is usually the first or second time until the participants get it), Jeff will gently tease the audience into participating by saying, "Can you do that?" It then becomes natural for the participants to listen for and respond to a question with an energetic, "ABSOLUTELY!"

> You can either ask them to type the mantra into the chatbox or have them unmute their microphones for three seconds.
>
> Make it okay for the participants to shout at their computer monitor! I simply say, "I know you want to say, ABSOLUTELY – so go ahead! Say ABSOLUTELY to your computer! We'll hear you! (or don't worry, we *won't* hear you)!"

WOULD YOU RATHER? 100

Perhaps you're familiar with the party game: Would You Rather? The premise is fairly simple: The player picks a card with a precarious dilemma and secretly predicts the result of the other players' subsequent open discussion and consensus view.

So let's riff off that game into the panel discussion universe.

Take two challenging, provocative questions to pose to a specific panelist. Put them up on a PowerPoint slide as Choice #1 or Choice #2. Then let the audience pick which question the panelist should answer.

Note: with a small crowd, you can just go with the loudest voice vote. Otherwise, you can use some kind of voting mechanism such as flags or online polling.

You might be wondering. What kinds of questions should I ask? Again, take a cue from the game:

- It's interesting.
- It could be embarrassing.
- It's a question we all want to ask.
- It makes us want to know the answer.

Inject a little levity into your panel discussion by asking each panelist, "Would you rather...?"

Use the online polling function built into the digital platform.
Preload your questions and have some fun.

101 HAVE A SENSE OF HUMOR

A seasoned panel moderator was asked, "Is it necessary to use humor in a panel discussion?" The moderator responded, "Only if you want people to listen."

Except for the guy whose car you just rear-ended, everyone likes to laugh. When you make your audience laugh, they feel more connected not only to you but also to each other. Research has shown that we like to be around people who have a sense of humor. It's a human quality that breaks down tension and resistance and enhances communication and relationships. Plus, it makes the panel more fun.

Now, I'm a person who has never considered herself funny. Humorists and comedians are funny. My brother is funny. Some of my friends are funny. But funny is not a quality I would use to describe myself.

Truth be told, some people find me witty, which brings a soft chortle, a gleam in the eye, and a smile to the lips. And I sometimes get a few chuckles from observational humor and stories that come from my own life experiences. I'm just not a laugh-every-six-minutes kind of speaker.

But I've found ways of strategically using humor that can help even the most humor challenged among us. Stop trying to *be* funny. Instead, find ways to engage your audiences with a humorous variety that involves them. Before you know it, you may even be described as funny—in a good way. Here are a few tips to make humor work for you:

MAKE IT NATURAL. Take the time to understand and appreciate your own style of humor. Stay true to yourself, and don't try to imitate anyone else.

BE RELEVANT. Make sure your humor supports the topic. There's nothing worse than irrelevant humor that distracts from the discussion.

BE APPROPRIATE. Use humor that is appropriate for your audience, is suitable for the occasion, and isn't offensive. While comedians often push the envelope with humor, a moderator and panelists should engage, not irritate, the audience.

ALIGN WITH THE TOPIC. If the topic is funny, then you'll be expected to use a lot of humor. Otherwise, you need to spread your humor throughout so it balances the serious material. After a panel, you never want to hear, "That was funny, but where's the beef?"

GO WITH YOUR HUMOR STRENGTHS. If you can do foreign accents or funny dialogue, then characters might be your strong suit. Be careful that you don't offend some group of people. If you have a knack for telling funny stories, then weave away. Though variety is good, focus on your strengths.

SELF-DEPRECATE. You're not only the best target for humor but your humor is unlike anyone else's. By creating your own stories and using self-deprecating humor, you create a style of humor that will make you unique. Plus, it connects with audiences because it shows you're not above laughing at yourself and thus not above them. A little crack in the armor brings you down to earth and makes you more approachable.

NUDGE YOUR NEIGHBOR 102

At any time during the panel discussion, ask the audience to talk to a neighbor or others at their table about the topic—and make sure the question you ask hints of some differing opinions.

For example, you can ask, "What are the misconceptions around centenarian nutritional standards?" or "What is the least nutritious food you have seen served to a centenarian at a facility? Could be yours or at another!" As you debrief the answers, you're already sparking some diversity of opinions.

There are three excellent times to encourage the audience to nudge their neighbor(s):

1. **BEFORE YOU BEGIN.** Ask them to nudge their neighbor(s) and ask, "What's something somebody in this audience should be asking this panel?" As you debrief the answers, the person speaking is reporting on behalf of the group rather than speaking for themselves.

2. **WHEN SUMMARIZING.** Ask the audience to nudge their neighbor about the most meaningful points that are most applicable to their work, and how they will apply the information when they get back to the workplace.

3. **AT ANY TIME.** Whenever a panelist says something controversial, you can ask the audience to comment to their neighbors on whether they agree or not.

Nudge your neighbor by putting people into breakout rooms of two or three.
Use this technique deliberately and sparingly.
By the time they get there, chat and then return to the main room,
it may not be the best use of your time.

103 PLAY BINGO

Many of us are familiar with the game, Bingo where a player matches numbers on their cards with ones randomly drawn by a caller. Why not play Bingo during a panel discussion?

My favorite variation on the bingo theme was used during the *Outlander* panel at Emerald City Comicon. At the onset of the panel, the moderator projected onto the screen a big bingo card with questions she thought the audience might want to ask the famous panelists. Periodically, she would pull a question from the bingo card or ask an audience member to ask one of the questions. It served as a sneak peek into what the panel was going to talk about.

HOW TO USE BINGO DURING Q&A

STEP 1   **MAKE A LIST**
Make a list of topics, phrases or interesting questions you think the audience wants to ask.

STEP 2   **MAKE A BINGO CARD**
Make your own bingo card, use a free online tool called BingoBaker that makes this super easy.

STEP 3   **SHOW THE CARD**
Project the bingo card on to the screen, hand out the bingo cards as participants walk in to the room or place a card on each chair.

STEP 4   **SHARE THE PROCESS**
Explain the directions during the panel opening:

- That you will be drawing from these questions periodically. Then, during the panel discussion, pause to select a question from the bingo card (or have a panelist or audience member select a question) and pose it to the panelists.

OR

- Encourage participants to note when a panelist mentions the topic or phrase. When they have noted the topics or phrases and have marked five in a row horizontally, vertically or diagonally, ask them to shout out bingo! It's always a bit of fun to ask the audience to shout out bingo! Then state the prize (or keep it a secret) for the first person who shouts.

STEP 5   **MODERATE THE PANEL DISCUSSION**
For fun, add a few random words or phrases and challenge the panelists to try to integrate them into the discussion. Don't worry about keeping track—the audience will let you know when or if you hit bingo! When the first person shouts "Bingo!", be ready with the prize. *Note: you may have the entire audience shout "bingo"—so be prepared to be able to give the prize out to everyone.:*

Email the bingo card to all participants and have them print it out beforehand.
You can even have them show it to you (and each other)
by holding it in front of their cameras.

USE SOCIAL MEDIA 104

When your audience is social-media savvy, you might use Twitter (or other social media platforms) to engage the audience during your panel discussion. Sounds pretty simple and straightforward, right? Just project the Twitter feed where you show only the tweets with the designated meeting hashtag and then you just pull comments off the feed.

Sorry. It's not as simple as that. You really want to think this through. Here's how I like to use Twitter, and you can use the same system for SMS/Texting:

First, since I want to focus on the conversation, I'll ask a colleague or support person I trust to be the ombudsman to monitor the backchannel of tweets or text messages. I give the ombudsman specific permission to interrupt if there are any issues or questions that need to be addressed at any time during the panel discussion.

Midpoint during the session, I'll check in with the ombudsman and ask, "What's the buzz?" or "What are people liking or not liking?" I'll also ask if there are any issues that need clarification.

If you can't find an ombudsman, you can periodically monitor the tweets or text messages through your smartphone or laptop. This can be hard to do while listening intently to the discussion, so think about taking a Twitter Break every 10–15 minutes to check the backchannel.

Then, be prepared to shift the course of the discussion and adapt based on what you see in the backchannel.

You can also ask a few Tweeters to step forward to share their tweets (both positive and negative) with the entire audience.

And if you're brave, you can display the backchannel on a screen that everyone (including you) can see. While this can be visibly distracting for some, and others will submit asinine tweets (Hi Dad!), you can respond immediately to any issues that come up. As a precaution, explain how you will respond to the Twitter stream at the beginning of the discussion, and they will be more likely to use it responsibly.

CASE STUDY
VIDEO AND POLL MASH UP

Daniel Anstandig, CEO of Futuri Media, was asked to moderate an important panel at the WorldWide Radio Summit. Panelists included chief executives from the world's largest broadcasters including BBC, iHeartRadio, and Cox Media Group. He reached out to me to make sure he was thinking through all of the elements to ensure his panel would be hugely successful.

First, we chatted about objectives and then we brainstormed ideas. Futuri and their R&D partner, the University of Florida, had a short video of focus group interviews with Generation Z's reactions to broadcast radio. (It's a hoot to watch.) So we thought this would be a good segue into the segment on Gen Z and technology.

But we didn't stop with that one technique.

After the video snippet, Daniel took a poll asking, "How many of you have heard similar comments from a Gen Z person you know?"

He took a look at the crowd and reported the results. (90% of the audience raised their hands.) He then launched into another curated question to one of the panelists.

Now that's a mash up using two techniques together! Just in case you were curious, here's the format for that panel:

SEGMENT 1
- Short video about Gen Z and Millennials—who they are, what they care about and their relationship with broadcast media.
- Welcome/set context/preview of the panel.
- Nudge Your Neighbor: First word that comes to mind when you think about Millennials and Gen Z.
- The Newlywed Game to Introduce panel.
- Moderator Questions: one customized to each panelist.

SEGMENT 2
- Video/Poll Mashup.
- Moderator Questions: one customized to each panelist.

SEGMENT 3
- Agree/Disagree Game.
- Moderator Questions: one customized to each panelist.

SEGMENT 4
- Video.
- Moderator Questions: one customized to each panelist.

SEGMENT 5
- Final Question: Most important piece of advice?
- Closing: Poll – How many of you got something valuable out of today's session?

CHAPTER TWELVE
MODERATE AUDIENCE Q&A

My belief about panels is that the moderator can easily spend the entire time asking questions that she believes the audience cares about...or she can actually let the audience ask questions that it cares about. I can't emphasize enough how important a Q&A period is; without one (or with an abbreviated one), it sends the message that the audience is there to be passive listeners, rather than active participants.

~ Scott Kirsner

QUESTIONS FROM THE AUDIENCE, otherwise known as Q&A, can enrich a panel discussion or derail it. Q&A is the quintessential method for audience engagement, but also has the most potential to go off the rails.

Decide ahead of time when and how you will manage questions. You can:

- **TAKE QUESTIONS AS YOU GO.** Allow questions to percolate from the audience at any time.

- **STOP PERIODICALLY AND ASK FOR QUESTIONS.** For example, stop for questions after each panelist presentation, key topical discussion, or every 20 minutes to take questions.

- **DEDICATE A TIME FOR Q&A.** Create a specific time to take questions from the audience, usually held at the end of the program and before the final summary.

Once you have determined WHEN you'll take questions from the audience, now you have to figure out HOW you are going to entertain questions from the audience. And that's where the pizazz comes in!

HOW TO FACILITATE AUDIENCE Q&A

At some point during a panel discussion, the panel moderator will turn to the audience and ask for questions. Most folks call this Audience Q&A where the moderator takes questions from the audience via text, question card, open mic, or Oprah-style, depending on the event.

To facilitate a meaningful Q&A session, a powerful moderator will:

DESCRIBE THE PROCESS. Share the process you'll use to solicit questions. Then follow it. Don't deviate for anybody (even the heavy hitter in the room).

REVIEW THE GROUND RULES. For example, "Please stand, state your name and organization, the name of the panelist you're directing the question to, your one sentence question and a few sentences to clarify your question if necessary. Please, everything in the form of a question. Now, what questions do you have?" You may also need to remind panelists to speak to the audience when answering all the questions.

REPEAT THE QUESTION. Repeat, restate, or summarize the question for the entire audience to hear and for it to be picked up on any recordings being made. Reframe tangential questions to be more on topic.

PROMPT A PANELIST. When the question is for anyone on the panel, restate the question and then direct the question to a panelist who:

- Is signaling to you.
- You feel would best answer it.
- Has not responded often.

DEFLECT THE QUESTION. If a panelist is not being asked questions by the audience, you can say, "John, that was a great answer. Mary, do you feel the same way?"

QUEUE. If a large number of people raise their hands, start with the first person who raised a hand and establish a lineup that lets the audience know who will go next.

FOLLOW THE QUEUE. Once you establish the order, doggedly follow it. If you have a hard time remembering the order, write it down or enlist someone to help you keep track.

ADD TO THE QUEUE. While a panelist is answering a question, you may see someone new raising their hand. Point to the person and nod, signaling that the person will be next in the queue.

CALL ON THE QUESTIONER. Call on them by name if you know them or can read their nametag. Otherwise, use some defining, flattering feature: "The lovely lady in the bright red jacket, please give us your question in one sentence."

WORK THE ROOM. Make sure that questions are spread among different members within the audience. Try to hear from everyone who has a question before you return to someone for a second turn. You can even offer that you are looking for new faces to chime in before you let a repeat questioner back in the queue.

PREVENT SPEECHES. You and any microphone runners should NEVER let go of the microphone.

LAST TWO QUESTIONS. Warn the audience when the session is drawing to a close and that you have time for one or two more questions. Take the last few questions and then move to the next segment on your agenda, typically, the ending activities.

When a moderator lays out the process and follows the ground rules, Q&A can be the highlight of the discussion.

DON'T HAVE AUDIENCE Q&A 105

Obviously, since you're reading this book, you can tell I'm a big fan of audience interaction during a panel discussion. So you would think I would be a big proponent of having a Q&A session all the time.

Au contraire!

There are times, when I do NOT recommend engaging in a Q&A session during a panel discussion.

MAIN STAGE. You have already seen the main stage speakers discuss the theme of the meeting or conference, and now you want to hear the interaction and interplay of these thought leaders.

AND

SHORT. Let's say the panel discussion will run up to 30 minutes in duration and you have three to four panelists. It just doesn't make sense, from a timing perspective—unless your panel is driven by the Q&A.

AND

LARGE. The audience is big enough that soliciting feedback within the timeframe doesn't make sense. How big is too big? I'd say 300 is getting too big, but it depends on the topic and the audience.

When you have *all THREE* conditions running at the same time, I would seriously consider NOT having Q&A during your panel discussion.

106   LIVE Q&A

Live Q&A means that you're taking questions from the floor. When you announce to the audience, "Let's go live. Who has a question?" the audience immediately perks up. Typically, they're going to piggyback off of the positive momentum that you've already created.

There are basically four different ways to get audience questions:

1. **QUEUE.** Questioners line up at the microphone.

2. **RUNNERS.** With a cordless microphone, the support staff runs to questioners who have their hands raised in anticipation (See Tip#44—Rules for Microphone Runner.)

3. **OPRAH-STYLE.** The moderator roams the audience with a cordless microphone to take questions.

4. **AUDIENCE TOSS.** Use a throwable microphone (I use a Catchbox), or in smaller groups, a nerf-ball or frisbee and have an audience member who has the question throw it to the next questioner. (See Catchbox case study at the end of Chapter 5.)

The key to a successful Live Q&A is to let all the participants know what the ground rules are for an appropriate question.

For example, you might say, "Please start with a one sentence question and tell us if you are directing it to a panelist specifically or to any of the panelists. If you must, but only if you must, follow up with one or two sentences. We want to get as many questions as we can in our short time together." By laying down these ground rules, you are showing the group that you are in full control of the session. Do not hesitate to reinforce the ground rules by intervening quickly.

One other thing: Depending on the layout of the room and access to the audience, it's a good practice for the moderator to hold the microphone on behalf of the questioner. I know, it's easier to hand it over to the questioner, but then that little window cracks open for the questioner to dispense with the ground rules and blather on. Do not hesitate to intervene and ask, "So what is your question?"

Your audience will thank you.

Q&A FRISBEE® 107

Want to add more pizazz to your audience Q&A during a panel discussion? Try using a foam Frisbee®!

So here's how this fun, and rather crazy, technique works:

Get a foam Frisbee® (or other soft, throwable object) and proudly show it to the audience. Explain how the foam Frisbee® doesn't hurt if it hits you. Demonstrate this by throwing it at one of your panelists or friends in the front row.

Then share the directions: "I'm going to zip this into the crowd. If it hits you, congratulations! You're asking a question. However, … (pause for dramatic effect) … if you catch it, you then have a choice:

1. You can ask a question, or
2. You can insist that the person sitting next to you ask a question instead.

Are you going to dodge it, or are you trying to catch it? What are you going to do? Alright let's throw out our first soft Frisbee®!"

And then you elegantly and effortlessly toss your Frisbee® into the audience. Once the audience member has had their question answered, have them send the Frisbee® to the other side of the room.

My recommendation is that you do this about three times. After that, it can get a little stale, so you'll want to use another technique to switch gears and ask questions from the audience during a panel discussion.

Obviously, you can't throw a Frisbee® into a virtual audience, but you *can* simulate the tossing of the Frisbee® ball, or microphone to an audience member by calling out someone's name. Give them the option to ask a question or toss it to someone else.

108 SCREENED Q&A

A screened Q&A is when the moderator collects, filters, and prioritizes the questions, typically on short notice. There are four ways to screen questions:

1. **QUESTION CARDS.** As the audience arrives, distribute preprinted question cards or index cards with instructions or prompts printed on them. Direct them to write their questions on the cards and hold them until you call for them to be collected. At a specific time in the session, ask the support staff to collect the question cards. You or your ombudsmen quickly sorts through the cards, selecting those that encapsulate key themes or ask an intriguing question.

2. **TEXT OR TWEET.** Invite the audience to text or tweet (or some other form) with the appropriate hashtag or cell phone number. Watch the feed while the panel is active, check the feed periodically, or ask support staff to watch it for you.

3. **SMALL GROUPS.** Break into small groups of three or four to discuss what questions they would like to ask. Pick random tables to ask their best question.

4. **SEEDED.** Ask trusted audience members to ask a straightforward or supplied question at the beginning of the session or during a lull in the conversation.

Caveat: There is a fine line between screening questions and censoring questions. I'm a big fan of transparency, so all questions that surface in the Q&A are fabulous opportunities to reconnect with the group after the event. Those questions that were not addressed can be addressed in a different format. So nothing gets removed. You just want to screen and prioritize the questions so the most relevant are addressed in your limited time together.

Censorship is when the ombudsman (typically a support staffer or someone appointed from the organization who understands what should or should not be addressed) pulls questions from the pile, never to see the light of day.

> Encourage participants to ask their questions in the question box, via text or tweet, or by putting them into breakout groups for small group discussion.
>
> The key is to have a deliberate strategy on how you are going to involve the audience in the Q&A segment.

DRIVE Q&A WITH QUESTION CARDS 109

Place 4"x6" index cards on the tables, each seat, or pass them out as people enter the room. My preference is to print at the top an interesting question that pertains to the panel, so people will instinctively know what to do with the card. Otherwise, they will look at the blank card and wonder what to do with it. *Note: 3"x5" cards are too small for people to write large and legibly.*

As people are wandering into the room, explain the purpose of the cards—that you will be picking them up and using them to steer the panel discussion.

After your introductory remarks, once again explain the purpose of the cards. Give them one more minute then ask them to pass the cards to the end of the aisle where your runners can collect the cards and give them to you.

If it is a small collection of cards, you can quickly sort through them. If it is a large pile, you might want to have one of the meeting organizers or a runner sort through the cards for you. Select the top five (or so) questions that appear most frequently.

Or you can ask each table or small group to chat about their questions and select the BEST question to ask the panelists. If the question has already been asked or answered, tell them to go to their next best question. By using question cards, you can let the audience drive the questions during your panel discussion.

You can also have an audience member or panelist pull out a question card at random.

Go the extra step and create value that extends past your presentation. Collect the cards after the program, compile the information, and feed it back to the meeting organizer or directly to your audience.

Even though the audience can't submit cards,
they can use the question box to submit questions

Consider using a crowdsourcing tool such as Slido.com that allows the
audience to submit their questions and to like their favorites.

110 CAPTURE THE QUESTION

Bob Pike, Chairman and founder of the Training and Performance Forum, shared this technique of capturing the question using small groups.

"I was told that participants in the Asian Pacific area would not ask questions and that asking questions would put them on the spot because potentially they could lose face. This has never been a problem for me in over twenty years because I have always used a participant-centered approach to presenting. I believe that the purpose of a question is for learning to take place, not testing to take place.

My participants are almost always placed in groups of five to seven in crescent-style seating—round tables with the front (the part of the table closest to the visuals) left open.

Periodically, I'll ask the group to come up with one to two questions they'd like to ask about anything I've touched on up to that point. I then give the tables a few minutes to discuss and generate possible questions.

Then I'll say that we have twelve minutes for Q&A and ask which table would like to ask the first question. There is always a flood of hands. I'll take the first one I see, answer the question, and then ask that table to choose the next table to ask a question.

At the end of twelve minutes, I'll invite them to post any other burning questions on a chart that I title *Capture the Question*. I provide stickey notes on each table for this purpose.

When asking questions, I will pose the question and then say, 'Your group has one minute to discuss the question and come up with an answer.' If it is something I have not touched on yet, I will say, 'Your group has one minute to come up with your best guess.'"

Use the breakout room function to randomly or deliberately place participants into smaller groups to discuss the questions.

CARD SWAP 111

One of my favorite ways to engage the audience is to ask them to talk at their tables or with their seat-mates about what questions they have for panelists. Challenge them to ask the toughest, hottest, most vexing questions they can think of. They can write their questions down on an index card or use Slido.com to allow the audience to like their favorite questions.

Here's yet another way you can ramp up the energy in the room. After the participants have written down their questions, ask the participants to pick up one of their cards. If they didn't write enough questions for everyone, then they can pick up a blank index card.

Ask the participants to move around the room and find someone from a different table to exchange cards with. These partners will pose their questions and provide answers to each other.

For those with blank index cards, perhaps the conversation stimulates a new question and then people can write that down on the blank card.

So here's the fun part: SWAP cards! Participants give their cards to their partners and you start another round. If you don't have time, direct them to take their seats.

Once the audience takes their seats, ask for the most intriguing questions from the audience. Here's the key to making this work: The people who stand are asking on behalf of the audience. It's not their question; rather, it's a question curated by the group.

The Card Swap is a fun and interactive way of getting people out of their seats, connecting with each other, and soliciting interesting questions for your panel discussion.

112 SEED QUESTIONS TO START

I just inhaled Chip and Dan Heath's new book, *The Power of Moments: Why Certain Moments Have Extraordinary Impact* primarily for insights into our ability to create magical moments for our customers, our colleagues, friends and family.

Oddly enough, I found a word of wisdom for panel moderators when conducting audience Q&A, particularly within a corporate setting where everyone in the audience works with each other. "When we have meetings, I typically have a plant in the audience and give them a tough question to ask," he said. "It's always a question we know people are asking and talking about but afraid to actually bring to leadership. I do this to 'pop the cork' and show that it's safe."

You're right to be concerned about people staying silent. One study found that 85% of workers felt "unable to raise an issue or concern to their bosses even though they felt the issue was important."

So get the Q&A started by planting a great, provocative question with someone who is respected in the audience.

CROWDSOURCED Q&A 113

Crowdsourced Q&A is when the audience drives the order of the questions. There are two ways to crowdsource questions. One requires technology and the other requires the participants to chat with each other.

TECHNOLOGY OPTION. As the participants walk in, encourage them to open the meeting app or go to a web-based tool. (My favorite is www.Slido.com.) The participants create and like the questions so you simply pull the favorites from the top of the list.

It works best when I preload five to ten questions that were curated by me and the panelists. No worries if those questions don't rise to the top, they get the intellectual juices flowing.

You'll need to have your smartphone or tablet close by or project the results in order to see the crowdsourced questions.

TALK AT YOUR TABLE OPTION. Ask participants to discuss the burning, relevant questions they would like to ask the panelists. Give them a couple of minutes to come up with their top three questions. Then go from table to table (or group to group) asking them for their best question, to be very concise, and to not repeat a question already posed by another table. If they don't have a new question, direct them to take a pass.

I admire the way David Robertson tees up his Crowdsourced Q&A session:

"You have the opportunity to set the agenda for the second half of tonight based on what you know, want to know, and what you've just heard. So stand up, let your blood move, and say hi to the people to your left and right. If there's a gap, move to close it. Then take turns to tell those people a question you think others in the audience would want to hear the panel's thoughts on. We'll give you five minutes to chat and come up with concise, challenging questions. Then we'll take five of those and the panel will discuss them for the second half of the event."

114 USE EVENT TECHNOLOGY

When you have over 300 attendees, it can be a challenge to get everyone involved during a panel discussion. Obviously, every person in the room can't ask a question—the numbers just don't work. And don't forget about that one person who may hijack the session with some obtuse, crazy question.

For larger audiences, you can use technology tools to enable the crowd to weigh in, typically to:

- Take a quick poll or vote.
- Gather questions to ask panelists.

Many panel technology tools are available. After canvassing the web, my fellow professional panel moderators, and my meeting professional friends, I believe there are essentially five different platforms:

1. **SOCIAL MEDIA.** Use a social media platform to drive engagement. For example, share a designated meeting Twitter hashtag, encourage the participants to post their questions using the hashtage and then project the results using a Twitterfall.

2. **TEXT-BASED.** Have your participants use their cellular phone to submit their questions or polling answers to a specific phone number. As a moderator, you can certainly give our your phone number, however, due to privacy issues, I don't recommend it. Try using PollEverywhere where the audience submits their questions and polling answers to a defined number. Since most audiences have some kind of smartphone, this can be a low-cost solution worth exploring.

3. **WEB-BASED.** Have the participants go to a specific website URL to submit their questions and polling answers. My go-to web-based program is Slido.com which is similar to a text-based option, but I find Slido is much more direct and less cumbersome for the audience to use.

4. **MEETING APPS.** Many conferences and conventions use a meeting app such as CrowdCompass by Cvent for registration, agendas and much more, so check with your meeting organizer to see if they are using an event app. If it has polling and Q&A functionality, I suggest you leverage the platform they are most familiar with.

5. **AUDIENCE RESPONSE SYSTEMS.** When you don't want the audience distracted by their phones and make super-super easy to take a poll, consider using a handheld device such as Turning Technologies' TurningPoint. You either invest in the hardware or rent it, and you'll want to think through how the audience will return the devices at the end of the session.

Sorry, you won't be able to use an audience response system
that requires a localized device.
You can still use social media, text-based, web-based, meeting apps
and the polling and question functions in your digital platforms.
To save time, set up your technology before the panel starts.

MOVE QUESTIONS ALONG   115

Sometimes, the question has been answered or it doesn't resonate with the audience. Sometimes, you just need to move to the next question.

Tim Mathy at Speak Inc. recommends this technique to move the question along:

The moderator takes questions from the audience via the meeting app and the panelists have one minute (total) to answer. If the audience wants more discussion about a topic, they hold up a green flag and they continue the conversation. If there are more red flags than green flags, then the moderator moves on to the next question.

Mathy's method is a simple and elegant format that also keeps the audience engaged.

> While participants won't have flags at the ready,
> they can give a thumbs up or thumbs down sign.
> Raise their hands. Hold up colored cards. Grab a colored item.
> Same idea, just using a different visual.

116 A, B, OR C Q&A FORMAT

You are conflicted. As a panel moderator, you WANT to involve the audience. You know that it's important and you want to keep people interested, but you really don't want to do a traditional audience Q&A. So why not give the audience an option as to which question they want the panelists to answer?

Here's how to amplify the typical audience Q&A format.

- Think of two or three juicy questions for either all of the panelists or for each of the panelists. This may take a bit of preparation, but all panel moderators should be preparing for their panel discussion.

- At the appropriate time in the session (perhaps about two-thirds of the way in, when the audience is expecting Q&A OR you need to vary the tempo of the panel), project a slide with questions bulleted as A, B or C.

- Ask the audience to shout out which question they would like you to ask the panelist(s). Go with the loudest voices and ask that question.

This audience engagement format is easy to use and injects energy into the discussion. However, you must think of the questions ahead of time. You can't do this on the fly.

> Preload questions into the polling function or share a screen with the questions bulleted as A, B or C.
>
> Ask the audience to vote by raising their hand or giving a thumbs up or down

HOT SEAT Q&A   117

When the panel discussion consists of top executives from the organization, it may be a bit difficult to inspire tough, provocative questions from the audience. Brian Walter, founder of Extreme Meetings, shares his technique to put the cards out on the table and ask the audience to come up with the hardest, smoking, squirmiest question they can possibly imagine.

And you're thinking, "*Huh!* The executives are going to buy off on that idea?" Yes, quite possibly. Especially if a core value of the organization is transparency or honesty.

To set this up, ask participants to turn to the person next to them and think of the hardest, most smoking, squirmiest question they can possibly imagine that is still professional and can be said on a recorded audio program. Assure the audience that the execs promised they would answer every single question until there aren't any left.

You think you've ramped up your employees' anticipation level? You bet!

Give them a few minutes to discuss. The noise level in the room will be off the charts! After time is up, you can gather the cards and ask the questions on behalf of the audience. Or, you can ask, "Which group/table has a really good question?" *Note, it's important to use group/table terminology because you don't want one person to be responsible for making the CEO squirm.*

Once you have identified the group, say, "Please have your spokesperson stand up and ask your question. Which panelist would you like to ask the question to?"

At this point, I always like to use my throwable microphone because it adds a new variable into the mix. The audience is wondering: How far can he throw it? Will they catch it?

Let one or two panelists answer the question, then repeat the process for three or four more questions, and then move on to another technique to engage the audience during a panel discussion.

Note: Some of these questions really ARE hot. To make it a little more palatable, allow the panelists an out by saying, "We're going to also give each one of the executives a get out of jail free card. At ONE time during the panel discussion, a panelist can say, 'I'm going to pass on that question to the executive sitting to my left.'" They rarely do it, but when they get a really hard question they exclaim, "Oh, I'm going to...Naah, I'll answer it." And we like them more because they have the courage to answer the provocative question during the panel discussion.

Rather than using cards, put the participants either randomly or deliberately into breakout rooms to discuss the HOTTEST question they can think of, and then submit the question (anonymously, of course) into the question box.

See how Brian Walter used this technique in the case study at the end of this chapter.

118 BRIBE THE FIRST QUESTIONERS

At a recent panel discussion, the moderator wanted to encourage audience members to share their failures in commercializing innovation. Not an easy task to get people to fess up in front of their peers.

"Hi! I'm Kristin, and I'm a failure." That's so not going to happen, so what's a moderator to do?

It all starts with the Why. Why do you want people to share their failures with each other? I presume it's to learn what doesn't work—which is equally as important as learning from successes. I love the quote attributed to Sir Isaac Newton: "If I have seen further, it is by standing on the shoulders of giants." The "giants" are the people who have gone before us—who have paved the road with their successes and failures.

Interestingly enough, another Why emerges when you talk to participants: "This conference serves as group therapy for those who have to actually commercialize innovation."

So we need to learn from each other and feel compassion for their trials and tribulations. Got it?

Now how are we going to get people to share?

In this case, the moderator gave away chocolate to those willing to share failure stories. You can have fun with it by giving out a PayDay or 100 Grand candy bar. If you have a flirty style, you could give out some Hershey Kisses!

Bribery works for certain crowds. And it doesn't have to be chocolate, either. But make it something inexpensive that everyone (okay, almost everyone) wants.

> Hold up a visual representation of the prize to the camera for all to see.
> Share how you are going to get it to them: Email? Snail mail?
> Make sure you actually *send it out* after the session.

HANDLE LAME QUESTIONS 119

Ugh. Sometimes, someone from the audience asks a lame question in a panel discussion. As the moderator (or a panelist), I believe you have two options:

1. You can either look like a deer in headlights, or

2. Reframe the question into a better question.

When the question is:

UNFOCUSED OR UNCLEAR. Rephrase the question close to the questioner's words and intention, but give it more clarity. After you have rephrased it, check for agreement. But then again, if you really have absolutely no idea what the person is rambling on about, ask the person to headline the question for you.

WEAK. Rather than restating or merely repeating a question, tweak a weak question to make it better than it is. Check with the questioner to make sure that's what was meant.

TOO SPECIFIC, DETAILED OR COMPLEX. Suggest the questioner talk with the panelist immediately after the session. "That's an interesting question, and perhaps better addressed in depth by panelist A after the wider Q&A we're doing now."

LONG WINDED. Firmly but politely remind the questioner to state the question. "What is your question?" "Get to the question, please," or you can be a little brash and ask, "Is there a question in there?" But let's say you're a patient person. Let the questioner finish their thought and chances are, the real question is lurking in the last spoken sentence. But then again, there may be *multiple* questions buried in there, so you may want to tease them out for your panelists.

A COMMENT. Intervene quickly when an audience member says, "I don't have a question, it's more of a comment." Briefly remind the entire audience that, "The panelists will be available for comments at the end," and then move briskly to the next questioner.

120   MASH UP Q&A

Why just use one Q&A style when you can mash it up with several?

You can start with, "Now we're going to go to the audience question part. We'll start with the first question that was submitted ahead of time." So now you start the Q&A session with a great question that makes the audience lean in thinking, "Oooooh, that's a good question."

Then you say, "Okay, let's take a question from the audience," and you run over to a live person and they ask their question.

In the meantime, you (or your ombudsman) is looking at the twitter feed and pulls another question.

Keep it moving, never using the same technique to get the question and keeping the audience on their toes.

CASE STUDY
HOT SEAT Q&A

Sometimes an interaction technique has value far beyond just the meeting experience itself. This was the case with a panel moderated by Brian Walter, founder of Extreme Meetings, for a global metal fabrication company.

After a series of financial issues and performance failures, the powerful plants in this company's manufacturing regions in Europe and Asia were openly questioning whether the corporate office and its leadership team were even needed. They began lobbying to spin off. So, the conglomerate that owned this company hired a new CEO from the auto industry to lead a turnaround. But there was widespread skepticism. This skepticism was almost palpable as the new CEO convened his first ever global leadership retreat with the top 200 company managers from all over the world. In addition to his speech, it was clear something else was needed to engage this leadership audience and establish credibility and belief in the turnaround. What helped? An interactive technique called The Hot Seat.

The new CEO invited his senior leadership team to join him onstage. He took the center seat. The CEO then explained that these were not just any seats but Hot Seats. It was their job to handle the heat. All GLS tables were provided with a bright orange Hot Seat card (with orange flames). They were instructed to think up the most pointed, relevant, future-oriented question they could imagine as a table and write it down anonymously. Nothing was off limits. They could ask more than one question per table. But the questions needed to be ones that would make the senior leaders sweat or squirm…or it probably wasn't a hot enough question.

The CEO then explained that he would read out every single question, without exception. Every question would be answered by someone on the leadership team or by him personally. To provide a slight bit of humor, the CEO gave each of the senior leaders one pass ticket. At any time if a question was too hot for them, they could use their pass ticket and the CEO would answer it.

The GLS attendees brainstormed questions at their tables for ten minutes, and then they were all gathered up and handed to the CEO. And for the next two hours he read every one out verbatim, including ones with colorful language. Often the question would cause a gasp to rise from the audience. But every question was answered…succinctly, bluntly, and with strategic candor. Mistakes were admitted. Inequities identified. Issues acknowledge. And paths forward articulated.

Some questions required lots of detail in the response. Others were answered with a "Yes" or "No". After two straight hours the final card was responded to…and then there was silence. The CEO asked, "Are there any *other* questions?" Silence again. "Okay, then let's get this done." Thunderous applause ensued. Plant managers and vice presidents from other regions told the CEO that this was the boldest thing they had experienced.

This single act of interaction and willingness to employ a Hot Seat technique earned the CEO much needed goodwill. It took two years, but the turnaround happened and they expanded their market share and revenues dramatically.

PART FOUR

MODERATE

— A —

VIRTUAL

PANEL DISCUSSION

CHAPTER THIRTEEN
MODERATE A VIRTUAL PANEL

Be very cognizant of your audiences. Some are live; some are going to be watching it recorded. They're not able to join us right now in this exact moment so they're doing it later. Make sure that you cater to them as well and be aware that you can have that hybrid audience of many different kinds. Think of all the audiences you'll have and address them as the moderator, as the facilitator. You want to be the one that looks into the camera and say, "those of you who are joining us at home, that are live right now, don't forget we've got this."

~ Terry Brock

UNFORTUNATELY, IF YOU DON'T KNOW the basics of moderating a panel in a F2F environment, then you won't do well moderating in a virtual environment. All the little things that a live audience won't see (or will forgive) get magnified online.

There are three different aspects to consider when it comes to virtual panel discussions:

1. **A VIRTUAL PANEL** is when the entire session (moderator, panelists and audience) is geographically dispersed and connected via technology.
2. **A HYBRID PANEL** is when at least the moderator and panelists are together in person and the session is live-streamed and/or recorded out to a geographically dispersed audience (sometimes called a blended panel).
3. **A REMOTE PANELIST** is livestreamed into the panel discussion.

In this chapter, we will discuss specific considerations for each of these situations.

121   THE VIRTUAL PANEL

When moderating a virtual panel discussion pay particular attention to:

THE PLATFORM. Get to know the platform functionality in advance. Don't just jump online on the day of the event and expect to master the system.

- Do a dry run *on that platform*—preferably with the panelists.

- Make sure the audio and video work for all and that there is enough bandwidth during the dry run and 30 minutes before the panel starts.

- Ensure there is adequate lighting on each panelist's face and that the camera isn't looking up their nose, which happens more than I want to report.

- Show the panelists how to log on, mute themselves (especially if they have a coughing fit), and turn the camera off (if for some reason they need to leave for a moment).

- Look at the backdrop. What do you see *behind* the moderator and panelists? Remove any distracting elements. (True story: I was moderating a panel and one gentleman had an abstract picture of a phallus behind him. Didn't even notice it until I watched the replay!)

- Learn the platform capabilities such as chatbox or polling features and then decide if you want to use them. If your audience is brand new to virtual panels/webinars, don't use every possible feature.

WEBINAR OR MEETING FORMAT. Decide which format you will use:

- *Webinar Format.* Preferable for audiences greater than 30 where *only* the moderator and panelists are visible and audible. Audience members may digitally raise their hands to ask a question, type in a question or chat with their fellow audience members.

- *Meeting Format.* Preferable for small audiences where the moderator, panelists, and audience are visible to all. This is a more intimate format where you decide whether you want the audience audio and/or video to be on or off upon entrance; whether you want each audience member to be able to turn their audio/video controls on/off; or whether you as the moderator will control this.

- *Ombudsman.* It's helpful to have others manage the backchannel—to monitor the questions, chatbox, and other social streams. Consider the ombudsman to be your eyes and ears on the audience. They are in a perfect position to alert you of an interesting question or to consolidate similar questions for you. Specifically, the ombudsman can:

  - Welcomes people and encourages them to start chatting in the chatbox. They can even strike up an audible conversation, depending on the number of people in the virtual audience.

  - Reviews all the questions, comments, or posts. Notes those that are mentioned the most, further the objectives, or directed to a specific panelist.

  - Sends the best/most asked questions, or those that will balance the airtime to the moderator.

  - Interjects the panel with a pertinent question or observation from the social stream.

  - Captures key quotes, ideas, and resources.

  - Cues the next person that they will be unmuted or video on to ask a question.

  - Clarifies a statement that did not come across well from the F2F into the virtual world.

  - Mines information and key takeaways to extend the conversation after the panel.

- *Technician.* For larger, more complex panels, have a technician or producer who manages the A/V streaming aspects of the panel and makes sure all the technology and functions are working.

RECORDED DISCUSSION. Some participants will watch the recording of the panel discussion. Make them feel included by looking into the camera and saying, "For those who are watching this at a later time, you can email your questions and we'll get back to you too!"

HAVE A PLANT. Ask a colleague to log in as a participant and get the chat rolling. Have them post a soundbite or takeaway into the chatbox to get the conversation going among the audience.

LAST MINUTE CHECK. Before you go live, make sure y'all look beautiful: no lettuce in your teeth, your face has appropriate lighting and your background is suitable. Remind all to turn off the air conditioner, the fan, the dishwasher or any other ambient noise.

MINGLE. Just as you would mingle with an audience, as people come into the virtual room, encourage them to enter their names and locations into the chatbox. You might even want to post a quick question for them to answer. And as you see the answers scroll in, welcome them by name.

NAMES. If participants' names are not displayed or unidentifiable, instruct them on how to edit their names. Consider asking them to include an identifier appropriate to the topic e.g. location, title, years of experience.

START STRONG. Online audiences get bored super, super soon, so it's crucial you take the time to think through how you're going to welcome the audience, introduce them to the technology and the topic, *quickly* introduce the panelists, and get right into the discussion. People do judge a book by its cover—otherwise known as the first three minutes. You want them leaning in so they stay riveted and refuse to multi-task.

SHIFT GEARS. Audiences get bored when the conversation stays between the moderator and the panelists. You'll have to deliberately mix it up. Do something as simple as taking a moment to look at the questions/chatbox or asking for someone in the audience to raise their hand.

STIMULATE CONVERSATION. Unless your panelists are extremely comfortable with the format and each other, they will be looking to you to *control* the discussion as to who should talk and when. So you'll need to be much more cognizant of the questions you're asking and balancing airtime. In an ideal world, you've coached your panelists to make it *as conversational* as a F2F discussion.

PERSONALIZE THE Q&A. Make it personal by not only reading the question but saying the name of the person who submitted the question while looking straight into the camera, "Reggie in Peoria, has a question about XYZ. Hi Reggie! Glad you're with us today!"

EXTEND THE CONVERSATION. As with F2F panels, you'll want to end the discussion with some final thoughts and a call to action. In a virtual session, you may also have some unanswered questions or great ideas in the chatbox. A great way to extend the conversation is to pledge that the panelists will respond to the unanswered questions within a few days of the panel. (Of course, you'll want to coordinate this with the meeting organizer and panelists beforehand.)

HAVE A BACKUP PLAN. Murphy will rear his ugly head. So think through what could go wrong and then try to prevent it from happening in the first place. Here's my backup plan for virtual panel discussions:

- Have all the panelists log on 30 minutes prior to the start time of the panel to check all the equipment.
- Teach panelists how to troubleshot various scenarios on their ends, including how to reconnect by calling in if necessary.
- Have the cell phone number of all the panelists just in case the video drops.
- Direct panelists to connect via hardwire and not WiFi. Make sure your panelists shut down all programs running concurrently on their computers.
- Have your panelists keep a pair of headphones or earbuds at the ready in case there is audio feedback.
- Have some interesting backup questions just in case there aren't any questions from the audience.

And don't forget to have fun. When you have fun, so does everyone else!

122 THE HYBRID PANEL

The hybrid panel has two audiences: a live, F2F audience and a digital audience. Typically, the panel is conducted on stage in front of a live, F2F audience and it is live-streamed to geographically dispersed locations. The virtual audience participates via a digital platform or may watch the replay at a later date.

Note: You may also live-stream a remote panelist to join the panel on the stage (which technically, isn't a hybrid panel, but is often lumped into that category).

It's downright depressing to see a hybrid panel exclude (or forget about) the virtual audience. I get it, it's easier to focus on the discussion in front of you. Moderating a lively panel discussion in the room *and* online is harder. Since there are multiple channels (in-person, virtual platforms, social streams, meeting apps are collectively called "omni-channel"), you will want to use an ombudsman and a technician.

As a panel moderator, you have to intentionally break the fourth wall to reach out to your virtual audience on a periodic basis. In addition to the ideas in Tip #121—The Virtual Panel, here are more ideas to make it easier on you and help your virtual audience feel more included:

HAVE A TWO-WAY LIVESTREAM. Not only can your virtual participants see the panel, but the panel needs to see who is watching virtually (or at least a representative sample). If you have confidence monitors (downstage video screens that face the panelists), project the audience stream to the monitors in the front of the room. That way, you and your panelists won't forget about your virtual audience.

LOOK DIRECTLY AT THE CAMERA. In your opening remarks, tell them how they will be encouraged to participate.

SHIFT GEARS PERIODICALLY. Create specific opportunities include the F2F and virtual audiences (see all the techniques in this book).

BE EXPLICIT. When tasking the F2F audience to do something, address the virtual audience and tell them what you expect them to do.

BONUS SESSION. After the panel discussion, consider having a bonus session with the virtual audience. Invite one of the panelists for a one-on-one interview or conduct a debriefing of the panel.

THE REMOTE PANELIST 123

The remote panelist is streamed onto a screen alongside the other panelists on stage. Seems pretty simple to do: Just get a monitor and Skype them in.

Oh, no. It's much, much more than that.

Here are some tips to ensure your remote panelist is able to seamlessly contribute just as if they were with you live on stage:

TWO-WAY VIDEO FEED. Not only will the audience want to see the panelists, but the remote panelist will also want to see the audience (as well as their fellow panelists). Set up a live feed with two cameras in the room: one capturing a close up view of the panel and the other capturing a wide angle view of the onsite audience.

QUALITY EQUIPMENT. Make sure your remote panelist has good quality audio, webcam and direct internet connection. Conduct a dry run with the remote *and* onsite panelists a day or two before the panel.

MEET UP. Ask everyone to meet onsite and online 30–60 minutes prior to the session start to make sure the audio/visual/streaming works.

AUDIO. Have the remote panelist audio run through the house system. If there isn't amplification, you may need to bring external speakers.

MONITOR. Place the monitor as if sitting on a chair next to their fellow panelists. Try not to put the monitor at the end (but sometimes you have no choice) and have the remote panelist at a similar height to the other panelists in the room.

SIGHT LINES. You and the audience need to have a clear view of the remote panelist.

- If possible, put the video feed of the remote panelist (or the close up of the panel) on the confidence monitor.

- Depending on the number of people in the audience, they may find it difficult to see the remote panelist on a small stage screen. Consider staging more presentation screens in the room so that everyone can see the remote panelist(s) comfortably.

PROPS. If using props, flags, posters, cards, etc., make sure you send them to the remote panelist ahead of time so they can participate equally with their fellow panelists.

BACKUP PLAN. Massive time delays (over two seconds) *will* happen at the worst time during your panel discussion. You have to do something to correct it, so it's helpful for all (including the remote panelist) to know the backup plan. Here's mine:

- Technician can mute/unmute the remote panelist to see if that corrects the problem.

- Technician can stop video/pause for five seconds/restart video to see if that corrects the problem.

- Technician can send a private chat message or text message telling the remote panelist to log off and to log back on to determine if that corrects the problem.

HELP YOUR REMOTE PANELISTS BE BRILLIANT

The audience knows when a panelist has just shown up without any thought or preparation. For a virtual panel, that lack of preparation becomes even more obvious. The panelists need to know the overall flow of the conversation and have several key points and takeaways for the audience. Otherwise, the conversation may degrade quickly. (See Tip# 28—Prepare Your Panelists.)

BE MORE CONCISE. Stories and examples need to be tighter and more concise. Headlines or tweetable soundbites are easy ways for people to remember what is being said and repeat it in the chatbox. If there is anything special or unique about the format, best to let them know beforehand.

BE EQUIPPED. While your laptop camera is fine, an HD webcam with good lighting makes for a better user experience. (I trained some panel moderators for Zoom, and they *demanded* I go buy one!) Same thing for your audio. An external microphone is ideal.

TALK TO THE CAMERA. Place the camera at eye level and in the middle of the monitor you're looking at during the panel. Yes, sometimes it does get in the way of your screen, but you're building trust with your audience by looking at the camera when you speak. When the camera is off to the side, up or down, it looks like you're distracted. (I suggest a Logitech Brio version on a flexible Joby tripod, a Yeti microphone, and a ring light.)

BE ADDITIVE. Especially in the easily distracted virtual world, the audience doesn't have the patience for panelists repeating what another panelist said. Encourage your panelists to add to the conversation. Rather than confirming "Yes, I agree with my esteemed colleague, [reiteration of what was said]," say, "Yes, good point AND [state your additional idea]."

CONTRIBUTE. In the F2F world, it's easy to signal to each other that you want to speak. In the virtual world, not so much. Even with high profile executives, our school conditioning kicks in and we awkwardly raise our hands to speak, expecting the moderator to call on us. So weird.

I suggest panelists lean in toward the camera to indicate an interest to speak. Or agree on a sign that indicates they want to speak. Then a moderator can easily move the conversation by saying, "[Panelist], looks like you have something you'd like to add."

WHAT TO WEAR. There's lots of guidance on what to wear in front of a camera. Here are a few simple guidelines:

- Wear a color that contrasts with your background. Just in case, don't wear green as it might conflict with a virtual background.
- Jewel tones near your face look best.
- Beware of wearing black, pastels, and pixilated prints as they don't show well in a visual frame.
- Wear patterns sparingly.

DE-CLUTTER. Even though virtual backgrounds are the latest rage, I'm not a big fan. I get distracted when a panelist moves and explosions of color erupt from behind. Take a preview look at what your audience will see—then just remove all the crap behind you. The empty glasses, the coffee cups, the dead plants, and other extraneous stuff that you aren't normally aware of.

SILENCE AMBIENT NOISE. Stop the ceiling fan, silence your phone, and turn off computer notifications. What about the household appliances, the dog, street traffic and other people in the room? They all contribute to ambient noise that can distract others.

Like all things, moving from F2F into the digital world takes a bit more thought and intention to be a brilliant panelist during a virtual or hybrid panel discussion.

CASE STUDY
A VIRTUAL PANEL

I recently moderated an hour-long virtual panel about the future of meetings using Zoom that went exactly according to plan (which is extremely rare). In preparation, I worked with the meeting organizer, Dana Saal, to clarify starting conditions and to talk through potential format ideas. Once we settled on our scheme, I sent an agenda to the meeting organizer for approval. Once conceptually approved, I then fleshed out more detail for the host and panelists so they could understand the flow and prepare appropriately.

Hopefully, you can gain some insight into this panel flow (which has been sanitized for a more general application).

Host: Name
Moderator: Kristin Arnold
Technician: Name
Panelists:
- Panelist A
- Panelist B
- Panelist C
- Panelist D

Objectives
- Describe how strategic thinking will improve future outcomes.
- List ways future F2F meetings could be modified to adhere to potential social distancing protocols.
- List opportunities for planners and suppliers to leverage each other's expertise for the benefit of all future F2F meetings.

Panel Agenda:
10 minutes to go: *As participants log on, Host and Panel Moderator are chatting about the question in the chatbox: "In 20 words or less, share your assumptions (you believe it is true or certain to happen) about the [topic]." Panelists are encouraged to read these comments and be able to react.*

0:00   **HOST - WELCOME**
- Why this panel? Why now?
- Quickly introduce panelists
- Introduce Kristin

0:05   **MODERATOR - REVIEW AGENDA/PROCESS**
- Provide overview of the panel and encourage questions (and comments) in the chatbox. The conversation in the backchannel may be just as interesting as what is said on the panel.
- Take Poll via Zoom – question with four options.
- Ask for panelist reactions/affirmations to the chatbox.
- Summarize into a few key messages.

0:15   **SEGMENT 1 - THE WHAT IF GAME**

Moderator to identify a panelist, then provide a question that starts with What If? Panelist provides a short response (no more than a paragraph) about what they could do, and selects another panelist to pick up the thread. The new panelist says "and" or "or":

- When the panelist says "and," they ADD to the original idea
- When the panelist says "or," they provide a different perspective.
- When the panelist says "but", stop them immediately and ask them to reframe their answer.
- Examples of What If questions are:
  - What if your venue can't accommodate your meeting specs under new social distancing protocols. What could you do?
  - What if your guests are unwilling to participate in a modified meeting experience? What could you do?
  - What if you move to a virtual meeting, but your speakers are not tech-savvy. What could you do?
  - What if your venue won't release you from contractual obligations. What could you do?
  - What if you can't have an opening reception. What could you do?
  - What if your meeting requires hands-on learning, such as a wet lab? What could you do?
- Attendees: please add your ideas to the chatbox. We'll be collecting ALL our ideas and sending them out post-panel.

0:30   **SEGMENT 2 - RAPID-FIRE SESSION**

Brainstorming session about [topic]. We're going to brainstorm different ways future F2F meetings could be modified to adhere to potential social distancing protocols. (No evaluation here, just making a list of possibilities.) Attendees: add to the list in the chatbox. Panelists: Come PREPARED. We will use the following order, so you'll pop off your answer after the person listed above you:

- Panelist first name
- Panelist first name
- Panelist first name
- Panelist first name

0:45   **SEGMENT 3 - DISCUSSION**

Let's talk about leveraging resources and ideas. Unique times call for unique solutions. (Come prepare to share your ideas.

- Attendees: Add your ideas to the chatbox.
- Discuss ways to leverage resources and idea.
- Check in with Host re: ideas in the chatbox.
- Summarize ideas.

0:55   **SEGMENT 4 - FINAL QUESTION TO ALL PANELISTS**

What's the one thing we should all keep in mind as F2F meetings return as must-attend events? (Please have several ideas prepared since we want to be additive and not repetitive in our answers.) Panelist identifies who should answer next until all have answered.

0:59   **HOST - THANK YOU AND WRAP UP**

CHAPTER FOURTEEN
VIRTUAL VARIATIONS

THIS BOOK WAS WRITTEN with live, in-person panels in mind. However, there are just as many opportunities to moderate a virtual/hybrid panel. This chapter is a quick reference list of many of the virtual variations noted in this book – all in one place.

MODERATOR CONSIDERATIONS
- Since a virtual panel is a much more visual medium, do not discount the importance of visual diversity.
- Keep an ongoing list (mental or physical) of who speaks and how long (short, medium, long). You'll notice the gaps and to whom you need to direct your next question.
- As the host, you also have the ability to mute, cancel video, or remove any or all of the participants, if need be.
- Be firm. Have only ONE prepared slide deck that you or the technician controls.
- If giving a prize, show a visual representation of the prize and share how you will get it to them.
- Use the ombudsman or technician to help you mute and unmute the microphones, recognize the raising of hands, and rummaging through the chatbox for the best questions to ask.

DIRECTIONS TO THE PANELISTS
- Most panelists use their built-in computer microphones. Encourage them to use a good, external microphone and turn off any ambient noise.
- Do a dry run and make sure the video is able to be seen and heard by all. If using two cameras for visual variety, make sure they (or the technician) knows how and when to switch cameras.
- Remove clutter from the background. The moderator might ask you to comment on something in the background, so know how to reposition the camera or take us on a tour of the room, office, or house.
- If using virtual backgrounds, test them during the dry run.
- If part of the program, provide direction as to the costume they should wear (style, color, etc.) or mail it to them. If debating different positions, encourage each side to wear something (such as a specific color) that signifies their unity.
- Beware of wearing the same color as the background or wearing green when using a green screen.
- Ask the panelists to keep their audio on and tell them the order in which you will be calling on them.
- If using a prop, make sure it can be seen by the audience – and whatever detail is important to see. Consider sharing the screen to show a picture of the prop.

AUDIENCE Q&A
- Have a deliberate Q&A strategy: Encourage participants to ask their questions in the question box, text or tweet, raise their hand, use a crowdsourcing tool, put them into breakout groups. Or have a plant in the audience.
- Form a queue where you identify one person to start speaking and let the next person know they are on deck.

POLLING

- Your digital platform will have a polling feature that you can either frontload or create as an instant poll.
- Use an external crowdsourcing app such as Slido.com or the meeting app to take a poll.
- Depending on the size of the group, you can get creative on different ways to take a poll. Ask participants to give a thumbs up or down; raise their hand, show a colored object, etc.
- Do a roll call of panelists or participants.
- Tell the audience that you are going to unmute the person whose name is called. Unmute that person.
- Drive the pace by clarifying the directions and then calling on each panelist in rapid-fire succession.
- Share a screen with the two or three questions bulleted as A, B, or C. To answer the poll, ask the audience to raise their hand, give a thumbs up, or write the answer in the chatbox.
- Post a continuum on the screen and ask participants to annotate an arrow as to where they fall on the continuum.

CHATBOX AND QUESTION BOX

- Have the audience type their questions into the question box and comments in the chatbox. If there is only a chatbox, have them type "QUESTION" in capital letters *before* they type in the question. This makes it easier for you to scan the chatbox for pertinent questions.
- Have the ombudsman monitor the chatbox and move any questions into the question box.
- Ask the audience to type their answers to a specific question into the chatbox.
- Use the meeting app or an external crowdsourcing tool such as Slido.com to show a word cloud as it forms.
- Save the questions and chatbox comments to reinforce key messages.

BREAKOUT ROOMS

- Place the participants into smaller, predetermined or randomly selected breakout rooms to discuss the topic and share their reactions/application of the information.
- Be clear about what you want them to do when they come back e.g. have a spokesperson to debrief the top three ideas, submit your HOTTEST question into the question box (anonymously of course).

PLATFORM DIRECTIONS

- To play music, connect your audio input from your computer to your platform. Don't forget to make sure you have the proper permissions.
- Depending on the audience's familiarity with the technology, you may want to give a quick tutorial on some of the basic features.
- Do a dry run and make sure your video is able to be seen and heard by all.
- Have the slides ready to be shared onscreen.
- Keep the virtual meeting room open after the panel for further discussion/chatting. Offer to place the participants into breakout rooms for further discussion.

LOGISTICS

- Mail any supplies (agree/disagree paddle, 8"x12" piece of white cardstock, thick black marker, costume, etc.) to all panelists.
- Email the handouts to the participants prior to the panel discussion.
- Email the takeaway at the end of the panel discussion or shortly thereafter.

CONCLUSION

EVERY ONCE IN A WHILE, I hear a drumbeat for an end to panels at meetings, conferences, and conventions. Many of these commentaries lament that panels are boring and don't deliver value. True enough, but that's not the fault of the format. It's the fault of the people involved. Meeting organizers choose a boring topic, a mediocre moderator, and/or pathetic panelists. When just *one* of those is a poor choice, I lament it too.

Recognizing that panels are ever present in the conference and convention world (in the 2014 Panel Report, 98% of the respondents indicated that they had seen a panel format during a meeting in the past 12 months), I don't think they are going away—even in the post-COVID19 world.

It is even more imperative that we make good choices to have great, powerful panels, greatly increase the probability that your panel discussion will be a home run.

My hope is that this book has inspired your creativity. It's not completely definitive, and I'll continue to add to the lexicon via my blog at www.PowerfulPanels.com. You can also:

- Download your free resources and checklists to help you structure your next panel discussion at **www.PowerfulPanels.com/BONUS.**
- Continue the conversation at our LinkedIn Powerful Panels group.
- Access our FREE (and who doesn't like free?) 7-part video e-course at www.PowerfulPanels.com. It's full of tips and techniques that professional moderators rely on. These short training videos will take you through, step by step, to moderating a lively and engaging panel discussion at any meeting, conference or convention. And, with your course registration, you'll receive several bonus templates and checklists.
- Listen to our podcast, *Powerful Panels* – available on Apple, Stitcher, and Spotify – where we opine about all things about the panel discussion.
- Subscribe to my YouTube channel to receive a weekly *Powerful Panel Discussion Tip*.
- Read my book, *Powerful Panels: A Step-by-Step Guide to Moderating Lively and Informative Panel Discussions at Meetings, Conferences and Conventions.*
- Unlock the Powerful Panels Knowledge Vault—a compilation of best practices of some of the most successful professional panel moderators. It's chock-full of customizable checklists, worksheets, templates, scripts, specialty format agendas, sample emails, PowerPoint templates, video examples of the good, the bad and the ugly, video interviews with industry icons and professional moderators, recorded webinars and slideshows, industry reports on the effectiveness of panels and more.
- Hire me to coach you to moderate a lively and informative panel discussion or to train your team of moderators.
- Or, just have me moderate your next panel discussion!

Please join me in my crusade to make all panel discussions powerful and extraordinary. And if you want to share a tip, technique, or reaction to something you learned while reading this book, I would be honored to hear from you at kristin@PowerfulPanels.com.

GLOSSARY AND INDEX OF TERMS

Airtime. The amount of time each panelist speaks during a panel. 108

Allusion. A brief, indirect reference to a person, place, or event that all can identify. 87

Analogy. A comparison of two things that are alike in some ways and different in others. 88

Audience response system (ARS). A methodology that allows participants to select or dial in a response that is then tabulated and displayed for the panelists and audience to view. 174

Autoresponder. A word, phrase, sentence, or gesture that the audience is prompted to respond with as a specific answer. 155

A/V. Shorthand for audio/visual. 65

Backchannel. The digital communications that occur during and after a live panel discussion. 161

Benchmark. The standard or point of comparison for all other panels. 10

Call to action. A specific request the panel/panelists make to the audience. 123

Closed question. A question that requires a one-word answer, typically "Yes" or "No". 60

Comparison. Where two or more items or ideas are examined for similarities. 87

Continuum. The sequence of adjacent elements with the ends extremely distinct. 95

Contrast. Where two or more items or ideas are examined for differences. 87

Conversational drumbeat. A constant reinforcement to the panelists at each and every touchpoint that you want the panel discussion to be a conversation. 110

Costume. A style of dress, including accessories and hairdos, characteristic of a period, place, or person. 93

Critique. A detailed evaluation or review. 132

Crowdsource. To obtain information from the audience. 173

Curate. To collect, select and organize potential content, such as questions to ask the panelists during a panel discussion. 58

Cutoff phrase. A prepared statement to bring an errant panelist back on track. 117

Debate. A discussion in which the affirmative and negative sides of a question are advocated by opposing speakers. 37

D.E.E.P. panelists. Panelists who are Diverse, Expertise, Eloquent, Prepared. 41

Demonstration. An exhibition of the operation or use of a device, machine, process, product, or the like to or with the audience. 50x

Escalating interventions. A series of actions a moderator can take to get the panel discussion back on track. 116

Example. A way to clarify or elaborate on your point. 104

Exotic. A panelist role that brings a unique perspective and experience. 45

Expert. A person who has special skill or knowledge in a particular field. 41

F2F. Shorthand for Face-to-face. x

Facilitator. A person responsible for guiding the work of a group to achieve a desired outcome. 3

Fact. A statement that can be verified, either by referring to a third source or by direct observation. 90

Filibuster. A long-winded panelist who takes too much airtime. 114

Fill-in-the-blank. A technique whereby the speaker allows the audience to complete the empty space or pause in the sentence. 155

Fishbowl. A technique whereby the activities of the panelists are open to the view or scrutiny of the rest of the audience. Also known as panel-in-the-round. 29

Format. The structure and flow of the segments of a panel discussion. 13

Handout. Any promotional or educational material given to each audience member. 54

Headline. A style used to encapsulate more detailed subject matter containing a few words. 155

Homework. Assigned work to be done prior to the panel discussion; also known as prework. 47

Hot potato. When the moderator asks the same question to each of the panelists. 106

Hot seat. A position in which one person is subjected to extreme stress or discomfort, usually with on-the-spot coaching by the panelists. 17

Housekeeping. Announcements that need to be made for the comfort of the audience. 80

Hybrid panel. At least two mediums are used to conduct the panel, typically an in person event that is also live-streamed and/or recorded out to a geographically dispersed audience. 188

Impromptu. A panel done without planning, organization, or rehearsal. 26

Improv. The act of creating and performing spontaneously and without preparation. Short for improvisation. 86

Illustration. An example that extends explanation or corroboration. 104

Initial remarks style. A panel format where panelists are allotted a short amount of time to present their perspectives on the topic. 13

Introduction. A short, personal presentation to introduce the topic and the panelists to the audience. 80

Lectern. A stand with a slanted top used to hold a book, speech, or notes at the proper height for a speaker or panel moderator. 71

Main stage style. Hard-hitting, short panel discussion with the keynote/main stage presenters with no audience Q&A. 13

Mash up. When you take two or more techniques and combine them together. 180

Media wall. A backdrop used for photo, branding, or award opportunities. 67

Meeting organizer. The person in charge of planning the logistical arrangements of a meeting, such as room setup, hotel arrangements, meals, travel, and other program details; also known as the meeting coordinator or organizer or conference planner, coordinator, or organizer. 3

Metaphor. A figure of speech in which a word or phrase is applied to something it is not ordinarily associated with, suggesting a resemblance to each other. 88

Model. A representation, generally in miniature, to show the construction or appearance of an object or concept. 94

Moderator. The person who sets the tone, the pace and control of the content of a panel discussion. 3

Movie clip. An excerpt from a telecast or full-length motion picture; also known as a video snippet. 142

Observation. A remark, statement, or comment based on something one has seen, heard, or noticed. 89

Objective. The end result that one's efforts or actions are intended to attain or accomplish. 8

Ombudsman. A person managing the backchannel in an in-person, virtual, or hybrid panel. 186

Open-ended question. A question that requires more than one word to answer. 100

Oprah-style. Where the moderator roams the audience with a cordless microphone to take questions. 71

Panache. A confident style or manner. 121

Panel discussion. A live or virtual discussion about a specific topic amongst a selected group of people who share differing perspectives in front of an audience. ix

Panel-in-the-round. A seating arrangement whereby the activities of the panelists are open to the view or scrutiny on all sides of the stage to the rest of the audience. Also known as a fishbowl format. 69

Panel meet up. A final meeting held 45–60 minutes *before* the panel discussion is to start. 49

Panel moderator. The facilitator of a panel discussion. 3

Panelist. A person who is asked to present a point of view in front of an audience. 41

Paraphrase. A restatement or rewording of a comment, giving the meaning in a clearer form. 100

Ping pong. When the moderator asks a different question to each of the panelists, but it always comes back to the moderator to ask more questions. 106

Pitch panel. A panel where creators offer their ideas to a panel of experts. 19

Pizazz. An attractive combination of vitality and glamour. ix

Polarizing question. A question that causes a division of opinions or beliefs between the panelists. 83

Poll. A collection of opinions on a subject for the purpose of analysis. 84

Pre-event email. An email that confirms the panel expectations, panelist roles and details. 48

Pre-event meet up. A short conference call or video conference a week or two before the panel. 48

Presentation style. A panel format where the panelists provide an in-depth sharing of the topic. 13

Prework. Assigned work to be done prior to the panel discussion; also known as homework. 47

Prize. A reward for winning or accomplishing a specific result. 124

Producer. The person who manages the digital platform and audiovisual streaming aspects of the panel. Also called a technician. 186

Prop. An object used or handled by the moderator or panelist in a panel discussion; also known as property. 94

Provocative question. A question that causes a strong reaction, sparks controversy or highlights a difference of opinion. 83

Q&A. An exchange of questions and answers between the speaker and the audience. 164

Q&A style. A panel format that provides ample opportunity to solicit questions from the audience. 13

Question card. An index card (or preprinted card) that is available for the audience to submit their questions to the panel. 66

Queue. A literal or figurative line of people waiting their turn to speak. 164

Quiz. An informal test or examination. 141

Recap. Short for recapitulation, a brief review or summary. 121

Reflection. The ability to give careful, quiet, thoughtful consideration to something. 123

Reframe. To restate an idea in another way in an attempt to help the audience understand and connect better with the idea. 179

Rehearse. To practice for a panel discussion in private prior to a public presentation. 109

Relator. A panelist role to cast that is easy for the audience to relate to. 45

Remote panelist. A panelist who is livestreamed in to the panel discussion. 189

Response cards. Color-coded index cards that create a visual response to a question. 84

Reward. Something given or received in return for something of merit. 124

Rhetorical question. A question asked solely to produce an effect or to make an assertion and not to elicit a reply. 83

Round-robin. A brainstorming technique in which the panel moderator calls upon the panelists and/or the participants around the room and collects their comments. 84

Runner. A person who is assigned the responsibility of carrying the microphone to wherever the participants are seated/standing. 73

Sage. A panelist role to cast that is a combination of Dr. Phil, Judge Judy and Yoda all mixed together. 45

Screened. Where questions are filtered and prioritized before being asked by the panel moderator. 28

Seeded. When a trusted audience member is given or asked a question to start the Q&A segment. 28

Segment. A specific section of the panel, typically Welcome/Introductions, Presentations, Moderator-Curated Questions, Audience Q&A, Summarize/Takeaways. 13

Shift gears. To add a new technique to change up the format, element, or energy in the room. 135

Show-and-tell. An activity in which each participant produces an object of unusual interest and tells something about it. 94

Simile. A figure of speech in which two unlike things are explicitly compared. 88

Site. The location of the presentation; also known as venue. 67

Slide deck. The file or the display of a series of digital slides. 53

SME. Subject Matter Expert. 23

Statistic. A numerical fact or figure that typically shows the relationship between the part and the whole. 90

Story-question. When you ask a question in such a way that the panelist is compelled to answer in the form of a story or anecdote. 105

Survey. A collection of facts, figures, or opinions taken and used in the preparation of a presentation. 153

Synthesize. Combine a number of things said during the panel discussion and bring it to a coherent whole. 102

Takeaway. Printed material, advice, or other gift that is handed out after the presentation. 54

Technician. The person who manages the digital platform and audiovisual streaming aspects of the panel. Also called a producer. 186

Theme. A unifying or dominant idea within the event. 8

Transition. Change from one segment or discussion thread to another. 102

Twitter. A free social networking and microblogging service that enables its users to send and read messages known as tweets. 153

UnPanel. A panel of four to five people without a moderator. 25

Venue. The location of the presentation; also known as site. 67

Video snippet. A small excerpt from a video; also known as a movie clip. 142

Virtual panel. When the entire session (moderator, panelists and audience) is geographically dispersed and connected by technology. 186

Visual diversity. The visual representation of the audience including gender, ethnicity and race. 42

Visual keepsake. A visible symbol the panelists wear throughout the event that signifies they were part of the panel. 51

Wild man/woman. A panelist role to cast where the audience has no idea what to expect from the panelist. 45

ACKNOWLEDGEMENTS

None of these techniques were created in a vacuum. I either observed them over the years or was inspired by others. Specifically, I'd like to thank these folks who have graciously allowed me to ask questions, probe into process, and capture various techniques for this book: Daniel Anstandig, Chip Bell, Terry Brock, Matt Dadey, Kate Delaney, Raoul Encinas, Ryan Foland, Sasscer Hill, Sally Hogshead, Sam Horn, Camilla Jensen, Scott Kirsner, Hugh Lee, Lynn Lester, Elizabeth Marshall, Tim Mathy, Scott McKain, Sarah Michel, Deborah Molique, Brad Montgomery, Randy Pennington, Bob Pike, Mark Sanborn, and Jane Stevens.

A big shout out to the brilliant Brian Walter, founder of Extreme Meetings who altered my definition of Extreme Panels. Truth be told, he inspired far more ideas in this book than any other human being on the planet. Thanks, Brian!

A huge thank you to my mentor and friend, Elaine Biech who graciously edited the book for content and flow. It would be a mess if she hadn't provided the clarity, perspective, and organization.

To Dana Saal who not only is an awesome association consultant, she is also an awesome book editor. So appreciate your diligence and attention to detail—and notice the correct usage of the em dash and my restraint in using yet another exclamation mark.

To my retired friend and neighbor, Susan Stark, who painstakingly reviewed my final advanced reader copy. My heart sang when she said, "If I had only read this book when I was a working professional. I had no idea you could do all that with a panel!"

A humungous hug for my husband, Joseph Sherren. He has patiently listened to me ramble about writing this book for so long...I think he's happy it's finally in print. (Although it will never be "done." I'm still collecting ideas. Maybe volume two?)

My biggest inspiration comes from you: the current and future panel moderators of the world. We desperately need to upgrade the panel experience and now you have over 100 ideas to add more pizazz to your panels!

ABOUT THE AUTHOR

KRISTIN ARNOLD, MBA, CSP, CPF-Master is a high-stakes meeting facilitator and professional panel moderator. She has been facilitating teams of executives and managers in making better decisions and achieving greater results for over 25 years. She is known for her concrete approach to teamwork and a treasure trove of practical concepts, tools, and techniques her clients can apply immediately to see positive, substantive results.

One of her favorite formats for helping executives, experts and practitioners share their ideas with others is the panel discussion at meetings, conferences and conventions.

She is a leading authority on moderating panel discussions, has been heralded by MeetingsNet as the *Panel Improvement Evangelist,* and recognized as a meetings innovator by Smart Meetings Magazine. Her article in Toastmasters Magazine continues to be their top-rated article and a lead article in organic Google search. She is the author of the definitive book on how to moderate a panel: *Powerful Panels: A Step-by-Step Guide to Moderating a Lively and Informative Panel Discussion at Meetings, Conferences, and Conventions.*

Kristin is one of the first female graduates of the US Coast Guard Academy and the first woman stationed onboard the USCGC Buttonwood, a seagoing buoy tender. She parlayed her understanding of teams and teamwork with an MBA in marketing strategy into a specialized management consulting firm focused on building extraordinary teams in the workplace.

OTHER BOOKS BY KRISTIN ARNOLD

Powerful Panels: A Step-by-Step Guide to Moderating a Lively and Informative Panel Discussion
at Meetings, Conferences and Conventions

Boring to Bravo: Proven Presentation Techniques to Engage, Involve and Inspire Your Audiences to Action

Team Basics: Practical Strategies for Team Success

Team Energizers: Practical Team Activities

Email Basics: Practical Tips to Improve Team Communication

Kristin's books are available with special discounts for bulk purchases. Customized editions with personalized covers and forewords, printed excerpts of existing books, and white-labeled products can be created for specific events or organizations.

Please contact Kristin for complete information
800.589.4733 • 480.399.8489
kristin@PowerfulPanels.com • www.PowerfulPanels.com
Please visit our site for additional content and frequent updates.

Follow Kristin Online

www.ingramcontent.com/pod-product-compliance
Lightning Source LLC
Chambersburg PA
CBHW05121200326
41519CB00025B/7086